I0470258

Suck It Up!

Strategies for effective leadership and motivation

by
Nathan Venture.D

Copyright 2023 Well-Being Publishing. All rights reserved.

No part of this book may be reproduced in any form or by any electronic or mechanical means including information storage and retrieval systems, without permission in writing from the author. The only exception is by a reviewer, who may quote short excerpts in a review.

Although the author and publisher have made every effort to ensure that the information in this book was correct at press time, the author and publisher do not assume and hereby disclaim any liability to any party for any loss, damage, or disruption caused by errors or omissions, whether such errors or omissions result from negligence, accident, or any other cause.

This publication is designed to provide accurate and authoritative information with regard to the subject matter covered. It is sold with the understanding that the publisher is not engaged in rendering professional services. If legal advice or other expert assistance is required, the services of a competent professional should be sought.

The fact that an organization or website is referred to in this work as a citation and/or a potential source of further information does not mean that the author or the publisher endorses the information the organization or website may provide or recommendations it may make.

Please remember that Internet websites listed in this work may have changed or disappeared between when this work was written and when it is read.

To You,

Thank you!

Table of Contents

Introduction:
Embracing Leadership and Motivation

Leadership is not merely a position or title; it is a journey of influence and inspiration. The essence of true leadership lies in its ability to motivate and empower others towards a vision of success. As emerging or established leaders, the exploration of this rich landscape begins with an understanding of the interplay between leadership and motivation.

Leadership is often misunderstood. It is easy to be drawn into the allure of commanding authority, but it takes profound insight to nurture growth and encourage progress. As you embark on the path of becoming an impactful leader, recognize that your capacity to ignite a fire within others, to propel them forward, is the cornerstone of effective leadership. It's about stirring hearts, igniting minds, and setting souls ablaze with purpose and passion.

Understanding leadership and motivation is akin to understanding the human spirit; it's complex, multifaceted, and inherently driven by a desire for connection and achievement. To harness the power of motivation as a leader, you'll need to dive deep into the psychological underpinnings that motivate human behavior. But beyond theory, you'll need practical strategies that translate into daily actions and interactions.

The motive force behind every great team is the unseen spirit crafted by a leader who understands their team's individual and collective needs. This spirit encompasses both the heart and mind, reflecting the dual components of emotional and rational motivation. When these elements are aligned, the potential for extraordinary outcomes is limitless.

Efficient communication is the lifeline of leadership. The way a leader listens, provides feedback, and navigates challenging conversations lays the groundwork for trust and clarity. Mastering these skills is essential because your words and actions become the mirror in which team members see their purpose and potential.

Goal setting, often thought of as a mundane task, is in fact a transformative process. It provides direction and sets the stage for accomplishment. As a leader, you must not only set clear, measurable goals but also inspire your team to embark on the journey to achieve them. The art of setting and pursuing goals is a balance of foresight, ambition, and realism.

Positive reinforcement is a powerful tool that, when used correctly, can lead to tremendous improvements in team performance. It's not about simple rewards; it's the nuanced understanding of when to offer praise and how to fuel ongoing motivation. Recognizing achievements in a manner that resonates with your team members is both an art and a science.

Leadership is not without its challenges. Obstacles such as burnout, disengagement, and resistance are all too common. These hurdles can dampen motivation, but they also provide a platform for leadership growth. Tackling these issues head-on demonstrates resilience and sets an example for your team to follow.

Fostering a motivational work environment is an ongoing process that demands consistent effort. Every decision, every interaction shapes the organizational culture. The environment you cultivate must be one of encouragement, where individuals feel valued and empowered to contribute their best.

Instilling a sense of vision and purpose transforms jobs into callings, tasks into missions. When people understand the 'why' behind their work, their engagement, productivity, and satisfaction soar. As a leader, it's your job to make that vision palpable, to draw the connection between individual roles and the larger goal.

Team development and collaboration are not passive outcomes of working together; they are the results of deliberate leadership actions. When you facilitate team synergy, you are effectively creating an ecosystem where individuals can thrive, innovate, and produce results that are greater than the sum of their parts.

Diversity in leadership does more than simply tick boxes on an inclusivity checklist. It brings together a wealth of perspectives, experiences, and ideas that can lead to innovative solutions. Navigating the dynamics of a diverse team requires a sophisticated level of emotional intelligence and intercultural competence.

Lifelong learning and continuous improvement are the lifeblood of effective leadership. In the ever-evolving landscape of business and human relations, stagnation is the enemy of progress. By fostering a growth mindset within yourself and your team, you demonstrate a commitment to personal and professional excellence.

Change and uncertainty are unavoidable, but the manner in which a leader faces these constants can define their legacy. Developing adaptive and agile teams is critical in an ever-shifting environment. The capacity to navigate these seas of change is what elevates a competent leader to an extraordinary one.

As this introduction unfolds, it becomes evident that leadership and motivation are inextricably linked. The journey you are about to embark on is not just about acquiring knowledge; it is about transforming that knowledge into action. The cultivation of these leadership qualities will propel not only your team but also yourself towards a brighter, more dynamic future. Embrace this journey with fervor and diligence, for the art of leadership is the art of human potential.

Chapter 1:
The Heart of Leadership

Embarking on the journey of leadership, one must first peer inward to understand the core of what it means to lead. Leadership isn't about authority or titles; it's an art that resides in the heart of those who inspire others, a skill born from self-awareness and the ability to connect with people on an emotional level. Grasping your unique leadership style is akin to unlocking a treasure trove of potential, harnessing the power to move and motivate. It begins with recognizing the pulse of your own motivations and extends to discerning the emotions and aspirations of your team. Emotional intelligence is the compass that will guide you to lead with empathy, to read the room, to know when to push forward with vigor and when to pull back with understanding. In this chapter, we'll explore how tapping into the heart of leadership can radiate authenticity and how, with this knowledge, you can foster a space where trust, respect, and unwavering motivation flourish.

Understanding Your Leadership Style

Leadership is an art, a kinetic and living process that evolves with every situation and interaction. To truly master this art, one must first gaze inward, to understand the unique spectrum of traits, behaviors, and tendencies that they bring to the leadership table. Grappling with, and ultimately understanding, your leadership style is not just beneficial, it's critical to your success and the flourishing of those you lead.

At the heart of leadership lies the understanding of oneself. The most impactful leaders are those who have done the hard work of digging into their own psychological backyard, uncovering the seeds of their leadership style. This introspection isn't an exercise in vanity, but a quest to unearth the framework upon which your leadership stands. It's about discerning whether your style is transformational, inspiring change and positive growth, or perhaps more transactional, focused on the mechanics of give-and-take.

Leadership style isn't a one-size-fits-all concept. Some leaders naturally adopt a democratic stance, seeking consensus and empowerment among their team, while others may lean towards autocratic methods, with a clear and direct approach. A laissez-faire leader could provide autonomy to their team, foster independence, and support innovation, whereas a coaching leader focuses on developing people for the future. Each of these styles comes with inherent strengths and areas for development.

Discovering your leadership style isn't a passive endeavor; it requires active engagement and reflection. This might involve soliciting feedback from peers, mentors, or team members. It means evaluating your responses to past challenges, your natural reactions to conflict, and how you praise and critique. How do you navigate success and failure, both personally and within your team? Your tactics in these areas are telling of your leadership nature.

Your leadership style also impacts how you motivate. A charismatic leader may spark enthusiasm through sheer force of personality, but what if your strength lies in empathetic listening or strategic thinking? Understanding your style will enable you to effectively motivate your team in a way that is genuine and aligned with your core leadership values. It's vital to comprehend that the same methods won't fan the flames of motivation in everyone equally.

Instead, adapting your approach to the individual can create a more invigorated and dynamic team.

Equally essential is recognizing that your leadership style will have blind spots. It's natural. What matters is how you address these areas. Are you too risk-averse for the innovative culture you wish to foster? Do you struggle with delegation? These shortfalls, once recognized, don't spell doom. Instead, they offer a roadmap for personal growth and leadership development.

Embracing your leadership style also includes the courage to evolve. As situations and team dynamics change, so might the requirements of your leadership. An adaptive leader knows when it's time to pivot from their natural style to best serve the situation at hand – a skill that's invaluable and often underappreciated.

Your team is a reflection of your leadership. Observing how your team operates, identifies problems, and celebrates victories can provide insights into your leadership style. Does your team feel empowered to take initiative, or do they wait for direction? Are they collaborative or siloed? These patterns offer clues to your dominant leadership tendencies and their impact.

Leader self-awareness is only the first step; putting that awareness into action is what makes the difference. It's about aligning your behaviors with your objectives and values, then consistently acting in accordance with that alignment. It's about wielding your unique style not as a weapon but as a tool of empowerment, to liberate the potential in each of your team members.

Understanding your leadership style means also accepting its evolutionary nature. Leadership isn't static but an ever-unfolding journey. As you progress in your career, you'll encounter new challenges and learning opportunities that will test and reshape your leadership approach. It's the leaders who remain students of their own style that find long-term success and fulfillment.

Let's not forget the cultural dimensions that shape leadership styles. Your background, experiences, and beliefs are all woven into the fabric of how you lead. Recognizing and respecting this cultural tapestry is key to authentic and relatable leadership. It's also crucial in a globalized work environment, where cross-cultural understanding can make or break the effectiveness of a leader.

Leadership is about people, and harnessing the power of motivation lies at its core. By comprehensively grasping your leadership style, you can tailor your motivational strategies to be as effective as possible. It is this match between leader and motive that sparks the outstanding performance, the unwavering dedication, and the extraordinary achievements within your team.

As you continue to explore and understand your leadership style, remember it's a continuous process. Be patient with yourself, and value each learning curve as it helps to sharpen your leadership skills. The most transformative leaders aren't those who have it all figured out, but those who remain committed to the journey of understanding, developing, and applying their unique leadership style throughout their career.

Understanding your leadership style is indeed at the heart of leadership. It is the foundation upon which you can build robust motivational strategies, forge stronger team dynamics, and lead with a clarity that resonates with your values. By mastering this understanding, you can create a legacy of leadership that not only achieves goals but inspires greatness in those around you.

The Role of Emotional Intelligence in Leadership

Leadership is not merely about strategic thinking and decision-making. One of the most transformative aspects of any leader's journey is the development and application of emotional intelligence (EI) in their leadership style.

Emotional intelligence, at its core, refers to the ability to perceive, understand, manage, and regulate emotions—both our own and those of others. An emotionally intelligent leader is attuned to the emotional undercurrents of their team, navigating through them to foster an environment of trust and productivity.

Consider a leader as a conductor of an orchestra. Just as the conductor must recognize and understand each instrument's sound to create harmony, a leader must be cognizant of each team member's emotional tone to craft a cohesive working environment.

But why does emotional intelligence matter so much in leadership? Emotional savvy facilitates healthier work relationships. It builds the kind of rapport that goes beyond superficial interactions, encouraging a deeper sense of community and belonging among team members.

Communication is more than the words we speak. An emotionally intelligence leader is adept at nonverbal communication—reading body language, facial expressions, and tone. This level of understanding can prevent miscommunications and resolve conflicts before they escalate.

Leaders well-versed in emotional intelligence expertly manage stress, not just in themselves but across their teams. They recognize the signs of overwork and burnout and take proactive steps to promote well-being and balance, retaining a high-performing team.

Making decisions with emotional intelligence does not mean leading with feelings alone. Rather, it involves considering the emotional impact of actions and decisions. Such leaders are able to navigate the complexities of organizational dynamics with sensitivity and assertiveness.

Emotional intelligence is pivotal in motivating a team. A leader that can gauge the motivation levels and identify emotional blockages within their team can create tailored strategies to enhance drive and enthusiasm.

Mentoring and coaching are intrinsic to effective leadership. An EI-driven leader recognizes that feedback should be constructive and empathetic, fostering a culture of growth, rather than fear of criticism. It's about elevating individuals, addressing their concerns, and acknowledging their contributions meaningfully.

Change is inevitable in any organization. Leaders with high emotional intelligence are better equipped to manage change. They understand how change can stir up a range of emotions in their team and work diligently to guide their team through the transition with open communication and support.

Trust is the foundation of any relationship and a cornerstone of effective leadership. By demonstrating emotional intelligence, leaders create a space where vulnerability is not seen as a weakness, but as an opportunity for growth and honesty. This, in essence, solidifies trust within teams.

Inclusivity is not just a buzzword; it's an imperative for modern leadership. Emotionally intelligent leaders value diversity in thought and experience. They strive to create an inclusive environment where every voice is heard and respected, leading to more innovative and robust solutions.

To pivot the focus inward, self-awareness is a key component of emotional intelligence. Leaders who are self-aware have a clear understanding of their strengths, weaknesses, and emotional triggers.

This self-knowledge empowers them to act with intention, rather than react impulsively under stress.

Cultivating emotional intelligence doesn't happen overnight. It demands ongoing commitment and introspection. However, leaders who prioritize their emotional development foster a work culture that thrives on mutual respect, understanding, and shared purpose.

As we venture deeper into the heart of what makes a leader truly effective, it's evident that the mastery of emotional intelligence is not just beneficial but essential. It is the thread that weaves through all aspects of leadership—connecting, energizing, and aligning teams towards common goals with compassion and understanding.

Chapter 2:
Building the Foundations of Motivation

With the heart of leadership pulsing in our grasp, we shift our lens to the bedrock beneath our feet, the profound catalyst of all progress: motivation. As leaders, understanding the dual essence of motivation—as both an internal flame and an externally fostered spark—is essential. The era's greatest leaders, those we endeavor to emulate, know that the cornerstone of a thriving team is a motivation that emanates from within, unshaken by external tempests. But how does one ignite this fire in the chest of each team member and maintain it against the winds of adversity? The answer lies in a thoughtful blend of acknowledging individual aspirations while skillfully crafting an environment that cultivates these intrinsic drives. As the architect of your team's foundation, your charge is to lay down the first stones by recognizing where each member's motivation resides and then curating the conditions that allow those intrinsic desires to interlock seamlessly with the collective mission. It's here, in this chapter, that we unpack the tools and cement the knowledge required to construct a robust framework, empowering your leadership to transform the spark of motivation into an enduring inferno of success.

Intrinsic vs. Extrinsic Motivation

At the heart of every high-performing team lies a pulse of motivation, driving each individual towards shared success. Understanding the nature of motivation is crucial for effective leadership, especially its two core types: intrinsic and extrinsic motivation. Intrinsic motivation is an internal drive to perform tasks that are naturally satisfying, catalyzing action through personal fulfillment, curiosity, or the love of a challenge. On the other hand, extrinsic motivation hinges on external rewards or factors, such as monetary incentives, recognition, or avoidance of negative consequences.

Intrinsic motivation, the internal compass guiding personal excellence, underpins actions that align with one's values, passions, and sense of purpose. When we tap into this well of self-motivation, our tasks transform into more than mere boxes to check; they become extensions of our identity and avenues for self-expression. Leaders who foster an environment that allows for autonomy and the pursuit of personal mastery will see their teams thrive, as members engage deeply with their work and show resilience in the face of adversity.

Now, let's turn our focus to extrinsic motivation, the external forces that often capture immediate attention. Suppose a promotion, a year-end bonus, or public acknowledgment is on the horizon for a team member. In that case, they might channel their efforts towards achieving these discernible rewards. Extrinsic motivators are powerful levers that leaders can pull to align individual efforts with organizational goals. However, reliance on external rewards may sometimes lead to a diminished sense of personal satisfaction and could deter long-term performance if not managed mindfully.

An astute leader seeks to strike a balance between these two types of motivation. By blending intrinsic elements, such as fostering a sense of competence, with extrinsic rewards like employee of the month awards, leaders can create a more dynamic and sustainable motivational landscape. It's essential to recognize that while extrinsic rewards can have an immediate impact, their effects can be transient. The thrill of a bonus wears off, and before long, individuals may seek the next incentive.

Contrarily, intrinsic motivation is like an ever-burning flame that fuels perseverance, innovation, and engagement, needing no external spark to ignite passion within an individual. The key to harnessing this form of motivation lies in understanding what drives each team member. Is it the challenge of a complex problem, the joy of learning, or the satisfaction of contributing to a cause that resonates with their values? When leaders know what stirs the hearts of their team, they can align tasks and roles accordingly.

Another critical aspect of intrinsic motivation is the concept of flow, a state where individuals become so absorbed in their work that time seems to stand still. Achieving a state of flow requires a balance between the individual's skill level and the challenge at hand, necessitating tasks that are neither too easy nor insurmountably difficult. Leaders can facilitate these conditions by providing opportunities for skill development and setting achievable, yet challenging goals.

Commitment to personal development is also instrumental when it comes to intrinsic motivation. When team members feel they are growing, learning, and advancing in their careers, they're more likely to put forth discretionary effort—an individual's voluntary commitment above and beyond what's required. Leaders who prioritize development discussions and invest time in mentoring their team cultivate a garden of intrinsic motivators, providing rich soil for motivation to flourish.

On the extrinsic side, neglecting the importance of aligning individual motivations with organizational rewards could be detrimental. For instance, if a team member values recognition more than financial incentives, misaligned rewards might not only fail to motivate but could also demotivate. It's vital for leaders to not only identify what extrinsically motivates their team members but also to personalize rewards to fit individual needs and desires whenever possible.

However, reliance on extrinsic motivation has its pitfalls. Overemphasis on external rewards can eclipse the inner drive, dampening intrinsic motivation. When extrinsic motivators become the sole focus, tasks are performed merely for the sake of rewards, potentially eroding creativity, initiative, and even ethics. It's a precarious tightrope that leaders must navigate, ensuring that external rewards do not suffocate the internal spirit which drives autonomous excellence.

In stark contrast, intrinsic motivation is self-sustaining, often leading to greater well-being and job satisfaction. When people are intrinsically motivated, performance improvement is a natural byproduct. They're not just working for the weekend or for the next paycheck; they're working towards self-actualization. Such motivation is deeply personal and uniquely powerful—it's the difference between someone who labors out of obligation versus someone ignited by passion.

Leaders, then, must become connoisseurs of motivation. They should actively listen and observe, engaging in conversations that reveal the aspirations and drivers of their team members. Do team members enjoy autonomy, mastery, and purpose—the three pillars that Daniel Pink identifies as intrinsic motivators? Are they seeking external validation or internal satisfaction? Ultimately, the role of a leader is to tailor their approach to the unique blend of factors that motivate each individual.

In an organizational context, leaders should not overlook the symbiotic relationship between intrinsic and extrinsic motivation. Creating a holistic motivational environment involves valuing contributions, advocating for fair compensation, and celebrating milestones, all the while nurturing a culture where individual purpose thrives. Leaders are the architects of such environments, balancing tangible rewards with intangible fulfillment opportunities.

The discussion now leads us to a pivotal question: How can you, as a leader, develop the necessary acumen to navigate the complex landscape of intrinsic and extrinsic motivation? It begins with self-awareness and a commitment to continuous learning about the human psyche and organizational behavior. Develop the insight to know when to offer a word of encouragement that fuels internal drive and when to provide a tangible reward that acknowledges effort and achievements.

Remember, a leader's mission is to cultivate a fertile environment where motivation, both intrinsic and extrinsic, can bloom in harmony. By skillfully integrating these two essential forms of motivation, you pave the way for a motivated workforce that is not only productive but also deeply engaged, resilient, and aligned with your vision for success.

Activating the Drive Within Your Team

In the pursuit of building a foundation for motivation, one of the most crucial elements for any leader is to activate the drive that resides within each team member. This drive is the intrinsic force that propels individuals toward achievement and excellence. As a leader, tapping into this wellspring of potential is an art that can transform the dynamics of your team and the outcomes of your collective efforts.

Understanding that every member of your team harnesses a unique set of motivations is the first step in this activation. It's not a one-size-fits-all situation; what ignites passion in one person may only flicker dimly for another. Your role as a leader is to discover and nurture these individual motivators, aligning them with the team's goals.

Creating a culture that values self-discovery is beneficial in this regard. Encourage your team to engage in self-reflection to better understand their own drivers. Providing opportunities for them to explore their strengths and interests can reveal hidden passions and areas where they can excel within the team framework.

Once these motivators are understood, goal-setting becomes a personalized process. Goals that resonate on a personal level with individual team members are more likely to be pursued with fervor. Craft these goals collaboratively; involving team members in the goal-setting process imbues a sense of ownership and accountability for the outcomes.

Recognize the power of autonomy. Empower your team members by offering them control over how they approach their work within the framework of the team's objectives. Autonomy is a potent motivator; it fosters an environment where individuals feel they can exert influence and make decisions that impact the team's success.

Blending individual motivators with collective goals calls for a delicate balance. It's about finding synergy between the drive of the individual and the direction of the team. As a leader, you can create this cohesion by facilitating opportunities for collaboration where individual strengths complement each other, working toward a common purpose.

Communication is a staple in activating the drive within your team. Open lines for meaningful dialogue, and ensure that every voice is heard. When team members feel their input is valued, their engagement levels tend to rise. This open communication also allows for the sharing of inspiration and enthusiasm, which can be contagious within a team setting.

Educating your team about the "why" behind their tasks can further deepen their drive. When individuals understand the purpose and impact of their work, their emotional investment in the outcomes intensifies. Link everyday tasks to the broader vision and demonstrate how their contributions fit into the bigger picture.

Fostering a sense of progress is equally impactful. Acknowledge and celebrate the milestones, even the small ones. This not only recognizes hard work but also reinforces the notion that their efforts are moving the needle forward, which can be incredibly motivating for continued effort and drive.

Development and growth opportunities within the team can serve as a key motivational lever. Create paths for advancement and skill enhancement. When individuals see that their hard work could lead to personal and professional development, their inherent drive to succeed is stimulated.

Resilience is a virtue that you will want to cultivate within your team. Challenges and setbacks are inevitable, but with a resilient mindset, your team will view these not as insurmountable obstacles but as chances to learn and grow. Equip your team with the tools and support they need to power through tough times, and they'll come out stronger and more driven on the other side.

Remember, activating drive is not just about ramping up the energy when motivation wanes; it's about sustaining an environment where the fire of motivation burns steadily. This requires attention to the well-being of your team. Ensure that workloads are reasonable and that the importance of work-life balance is acknowledged and practiced.

Peer recognition is often overlooked, yet it can be profoundly influential. Encourage team members to recognize each other's achievements and skills. A culture of appreciation and respect can significantly elevate motivation and drive as members feel valued by their own cohorts.

As the leader of your team, your drive is as crucial as that of any team member. Your enthusiasm, commitment, and drive are powerful catalysts for others. By modeling motivation and passion in your role, you set a high bar and serve as a living example of what it means to be driven toward excellence.

In conclusion, to activate the drive within your team, you must weave together a comprehensive approach that includes understanding individual motivators, personalized goal-setting, fostering autonomy, creating cohesive team objectives, encouraging open communication, emphasizing purpose, celebrating progress, creating development opportunities, imbuing resilience, managing work-life balance, promoting peer recognition, and leading by example. In doing so, you'll ignite a powerful force within your team that can achieve remarkable results.

Chapter 3:
Communication: The Leader's Tool

Empowerment and clarity flow from the wellspring of clear communication, the mark of an effective leader. This chapter introduces the art of communicating with purpose and poise, going beyond mere words to the heart of interaction. You'll learn that how you listen can transform your leadership, creating a bridge of understanding between you and those you lead. Discover the secrets to navigating the turbulent waters of difficult discussions with grace and authority, equipping you for those inevitable moments when conflict resolution is key. Embrace the power of dialogue as a tool not just to instruct, but to inspire and engage the spirits of your team. It's about honing your message, aligning your non-verbal cues with your intent, and most vitally, fostering an environment where every voice finds the space to resonate. The pillars of strong leadership stand on the foundation of robust communication. Let's delve into how you can harness this formidable tool to unleash potential and kindle the flames of shared success.

Mastering Effective Listening

Leadership is an art, and effective communication serves as the vibrant colors on the leader's palette. Listening, a critical yet often undervalued component of communication, is where true connection begins. The capacity to listen effectively is where ideas flourish, concerns are validated, and trust is built. As a leader eager to motivate, it's crucial to understand that listening isn't merely a passive activity—it's a dynamic process that demands your full presence.

Understanding the distinction between hearing and listening is our starting point. Hearing is the physiological aspect—sound waves hitting the eardrums—while listening involves a conscious choice to focus on understanding the speaker's message. It's not just about the words being said, but also the emotions and intentions behind them. How often have you felt truly heard? That sensation is what you aim to give to your team.

Becoming a master of effective listening requires conscious practice. Begin by silencing the inner dialogue that often disrupts your ability to fully engage. When someone is speaking, resist the urge to formulate a response before they've finished. This is more than a courteous gesture; it allows space for the speaker's full message and nuances to unfurl, granting you deeper insight into their perspective.

Eye contact can anchor you in the present moment and fortify the bridge between speaker and listener. It conveys to the speaker that they have your undivided attention. However, remember that effective listening extends beyond visual cues and into the realm of empathy. Strive to grasp the underlying message by putting yourself in the speaker's shoes, sensing the conversation's emotional undertones.

Openness is a pillar of effective listening. A leader's willingness to receive feedback or divergent viewpoints without immediate judgment enhances dialogue and fosters an environment where individuals feel valued. This openness isn't indicative of weakness but of strength and confidence. It invites a multifaceted view of situations, which is essential for wise decision-making.

Questions are a listener's tool for clarity and deeper understanding. Asking questions demonstrates active engagement and shows that you are not only hearing but processing the information. Ensure your inquiries are open-ended and reflective, inviting elaboration that could reveal insights you might not have considered otherwise.

Part of effective listening involves recognizing nonverbal communication. Body language, facial expressions, and tone of voice can sometimes convey more than words. Be attuned to these cues; they often tell a story just as potent as the verbal narrative. Nonverbal signals can guide a leader to the heart of the matter, spotlighting areas that may need extra attention.

Listening must be met with acknowledgment. A simple nod or verbal affirmation can reassure the speaker that their message is being received. This acknowledgment, however, needs to transition into action for true validation. Following up on a conversation with relevant actions shows that you didn't just listen—you cared enough to respond and to incorporate what you learned into collective progress.

While group settings are a common venue for leadership communication, effective listening shines when personalized. One-on-one conversations can provide a treasure trove of insight into individual team members. These interactions allow you to tailor your leadership approach, foster individual motivation, and spot opportunities to help each member align their personal goals with the team's vision.

Avoiding interruptions is a cornerstone of mastering effective listening. Resist the urge to interject or finish someone's sentences. Such habits can shut down open communication and subconsciously convey that a person's input isn't valuable. By exercising patience, you honor the speaker's contributions and affirm their role in the conversation.

Consider listening a form of intellectual humility. Admitting that you don't have all the answers and that others might provide perspectives you haven't contemplated is powerful. This notion doesn't undermine your leadership; it strengthens it by diversifying the sources of knowledge and expertise within your team.

Mastering effective listening also implies adapting to different communication styles. Some team members may be succinct and direct, while others are more narrative and expressive. As a leader, adjusting your listening approach to match these varying styles shows respect for individual expression and promotes more harmonious interactions.

Effective listening breeds loyalty and trust. When your team feels heard, they are more likely to reciprocate with open communication, resilience, and dedication. It sets a precedent for a culture where transparency and thoughtfulness drive collaborative efforts and, ultimately, yield success.

At times, effective listening will necessitate having the courage to encounter difficult truths. Be prepared to have your preconceptions challenged and to face uncomfortable feedback. Embracing these moments with grace and openness rather than defensiveness can lead to transformative insights and strengthen the resolve of your team.

In cultivating the art of effective listening, you lay the groundwork for a leadership style that's as attuned to nuance as it is to action. Each conversation is an opportunity—an opening to inspire, to guide, and to connect. Remember, it's through the myriad of voices that the symphony of a truly motivated team is composed. Dedicate time daily to nurture this skill, and watch as it becomes a catalyst for motivation, collaboration, and flourishing leadership within your organization.

Navigating Difficult Conversations

As leaders, one of the most daunting tasks can be conducting difficult conversations. These are the discussions fraught with emotional undercurrents, varying opinions, and potentially significant ramifications for team dynamics and performance. Yet, they are unavoidable and necessary for sustained leadership and organizational health.

The key to navigating these conversations effectively lies in approaching them with a blend of empathy, clarity, and resolve. The strategic leader must balance compassionate understanding of team members' feelings with the responsibility of addressing issues directly and constructively.

It's essential to recognize that difficult conversations often stem from conflict or disagreement. The best leaders don't shirk from these moments; instead, they step confidently into the fray, armed with active listening skills, patience, and the goal of reaching mutual understanding and resolution.

Before diving into a challenging discourse, it's vital to ensure that you are well-prepared. Familiarize yourself with all aspects of the issue at hand and consider the perspectives of all stakeholders involved. This will enable you to articulate the core issues without getting sidelined by tangential details.

When initiating the conversation, setting a respectful, confidential, and neutral environment is imperative. Begin by stating your intentions clearly and reaffirm your commitment to a positive outcome for all parties. A leader sets the tone; therefore, being calm and composed, even when facing emotionally charged subjects, will help keep the dialogue productive.

Use "I" statements to express your perspective, as in, "I feel that..." or "I've observed that..." This phrasing keeps you from inadvertently placing blame, thus reducing the likelihood of defensive reactions. It's about identifying the problem, not the person.

Empathetic listening is your greatest ally in these moments. Give the other person the time and space to share their thoughts and feelings. Validate them by summarizing their points to show that you truly hear and understand them. This act of validation doesn't necessarily mean agreement, but it does communicate respect.

Avoid the tendency to jump to conclusions or solutions too quickly. Sometimes, the act of talking through the issue can reveal underlying concerns that were not initially apparent. Acknowledge the difficulty of the conversation and remind participants that tackling hard subjects is how the team will grow stronger.

In your role as a leader, be mindful of your nonverbal cues. Your body language, facial expressions, and tone of voice send powerful messages. Make sure they're in alignment with your words – showing openness and conciliation rather than confrontation.

Maintain focus on the issue, not the individuals. Avoiding personal attacks and sticking to the facts builds trust in your leadership and in the process being undertaken. It also keeps the conversation centered on a pathway to resolution rather than devolving into unproductive conflict.

When it becomes clear that emotions are running high, don't hesitate to take a break. Suggesting a cooling-off period before continuing the discussion can prevent exchanges from turning counterproductive. It shows your awareness and consideration for everyone's ability to remain constructive.

As you work toward resolving the matter, collaborate with those involved to find solutions. Empowerment is key — when team members take part in creating the solution, they're more invested in the outcome and the issue's remediation.

After the discussion, reflect on the conversation. What went well? What could you, as a leader, do better next time? Difficult conversations are rich learning opportunities to refine your approach and improve your effectiveness as a leader.

Finally, follow up on the conversation to ensure that agreed actions are being taken and that the issue doesn't remain unresolved. Your team will respect and appreciate that you've taken their concerns seriously and are dedicated to sustaining a healthy working environment.

Navigating difficult conversations won't be easy – nothing worth doing ever is. However, by approaching these dialogues with intention, compassion, and focus, they become not just hurdles to overcome but bridges to deeper understanding and better team cohesion. Your role as a leader is to guide these conversations towards constructive outcomes, fostering a culture of open communication and unwavering mutual respect.

Chapter 4:
Setting and Achieving Goals

Having honed a deep understanding of leadership styles, the weaving of motivation into the team fabric, and the art of communication, we turn our focus to the cornerstone of purposeful action: setting and achieving goals. This chapter is the crux where vision translates into tangible results. Leaders should embrace the craft of sculpting goals with precision, ensuring they're not just attainable, but also resonant with the collective heartbeat of their team. A goal, after all, is the north star guiding a ship through the darkest night—it must be bright, compelling, and clear. It's paramount that as a leader, one becomes adept at charting the course from the inception of a goal to its triumphant realization, giving due diligence to the creation of pathways that are flexible yet robust, allowing space for individual growth while precincting steadfast progression. As we embark on this chapter, let's armor ourselves with strategies that not only aim for the stars but also set in motion the steps that make that celestial reach possible. Achieve mastery in goal-setting and you'll watch as your team transforms aspirations into reality, empowering each member to surpass their personal bests while collectively reaching unprecedented heights.

SMART Goals for Leaders and Teams

Embarking on a leadership journey requires more than vision; it requires a roadmap. Most importantly, it necessitates practical, achievable goals that inspire action. Leaders and teams thrive under a shared sense of purpose and clear objectives, and nothing provides clarity like SMART goals. SMART is an acronym for Specific, Measurable, Achievable, Relevant, and Time-based, a criterion that transforms vague aspirations into actionable steps with clear metrics of success.

To set SMART goals, leaders must first be specific. This begins with articulating what exactly needs to be accomplished, who is involved, where it will take place, and which resources are required. For instance, rather than a broad goal like 'increase sales', a SMART goal would state 'increase sales of product X by 15% in the Northeast region by the end of Q2, using additional targeted advertising and increased retail partnerships'.

The second component, measurability, adds a quantifiable aspect to the goal. It's not just about increasing sales, but by how much. By setting benchmarks, both leaders and their teams can track their progress, remain motivated, and adjust strategies as needed.

Setting achievable goals is crucial. If a goal is too far out of reach, it can demoralize a team and lead to disengagement. As a leader, ensure that the goals challenge your team but remain possible with a concerted effort. This balance stimulates growth without leading to burnout or frustration.

Relevance ensures that the goal aligns with the broader business objectives and values. It must matter to those involved and bring them closer to the strategic vision of the organization. A relevant goal resonates, creates meaning, and encourages commitment from the team.

Lastly, adding a time frame introduces urgency and prompts action. Whether it's a deadline for a project or a quarterly target, having a time component discourages procrastination and facilitates planning.

A leader must not only set SMART goals but also effectively communicate them. When a team understands and buys into a goal, their collective drive propels them forward. Make sure to explain the 'why' behind each goal, forging an intrinsic connection between individual team members' work and the team's broader achievements.

Moreover, leaders should involve their teams in the goal-setting process as much as possible. When individuals contribute to the creation of goals, they feel a sense of ownership and accountability. This collaborative approach fosters a deeper sense of commitment and empowerment amongst team members which is vital for collective success.

After setting the goals, leaders should establish regular check-ins to monitor progress. These checkpoints serve as opportunities for feedback and course correction. They keep the team aligned and focus on overcoming any barriers that may arise. Remember, goals are not set in stone; they are living targets that can be adapted as circumstances change.

SMART goals also enable leaders to recognize and celebrate milestones. Every achieved benchmark is an opportunity for a team to see the fruits of its labor, providing a moment of reflection and positive reinforcement. This boosts morale and keeps motivation high.

For leaders themselves, SMART goals are personal commitments to professional development and excellence. Through setting an example and personal adherence to these goal-setting principles, leaders inspire their teams. They exemplify the discipline, focus, and strategic thinking that make the achievement of complex objectives attainable.

At times, goals may be missed, and that's part of the leadership journey. When setbacks occur, it's the leader's responsibility to facilitate a constructive analysis of what went wrong. This isn't for assigning blame, but for learning and improving. A true leader turns these moments into powerful lessons for future pursuits.

Furthermore, SMART goals should not only encompass immediate tactical initiatives but also strategic long-term growth both for the organization and team members. Leaders need to balance the pressing needs of the here and now with the aspirations of tomorrow.

In conclusion, setting SMART goals is a transformative process that instills purpose, clarity, and focus in both leaders and teams. It's about breaking down the monumental into the manageable, transforming the intangible into the concrete, and shifting from idly dreaming to actively achieving. Through SMART goals, leaders can steer their teams through the choppy waters of uncertainty and change toward the shores of success and fulfillment.

As you continue to lead and motivate, use SMART goals as your foundation. Let them be the stepping stones upon which you and your team tread on the path to greatness. Remember that each goal achieved is a testament to your leadership and the collective power of a motivated team.

In your hands lies the power to not only dream of a better future but to methodically carve it out, one SMART goal at a time. Seize that power with conviction, and watch as your leadership transforms potential into reality, and ambitions into achievements.

Keeping the Momentum: Monitoring Progress

Having set well-defined, strategic goals is the map to success; monitoring the progress is the compass that keeps one on course. It's about creating a dynamic wherein each milestone reached is a celebrated victory, propelling leaders and teams forward with vigor. Just as a ship captain does not simply set a course but continually checks the ship's position against the elements, effective leaders continually track progress towards their team's goals.

Momentum is subtle yet powerful. Picture a train gradually picking up speed; with each turn of the wheels, it becomes more difficult to stop. The same principle applies to teams and individuals as they work towards objectives. By measuring and recognizing the incremental achievements, leaders stimulate focus, enthusiasm, and persistence within their teams, keeping that figurative train moving smoothly along its tracks.

Initiating a rhythm of regular check-ins creates transparency and accountability. These scheduled pivots are more than mere status reports; they are opportunities to recalibrate, celebrate small wins, and learn from the journey thus far. They foster engagement and provide the team with an enduring sense of direction and purpose. When progress is tracked and communicated effectively, it bridges the gap between start and accomplishment.

Leaders must also be dexterous in their response to the information gained from monitoring. Data, after all, are rich with insights. Sometimes goals need adjusting because the initial assumptions change. Perhaps the market shifts, or resources become limited. It is then the leader's task to adjust the sails, keeping the goals ambitious yet achievable within the new parameters. Agility in leadership is not about abandoning course but about intelligent and informed steering.

In the landscape of goal achievement, feedback is the rainfall that nurtures growth. It's not enough to set a goal and forget it; like a garden, it needs consistent tending. This includes gathering feedback from all relevant sources—team members, clients, stakeholders—and employing it to strengthen the strategy. Moreover, feedback should be a two-way dialogue, ensuring that voices from every level contribute to the collective effort.

Yet, tracking progress is not merely an analytical task but a ritual that can instill a sense of accomplishment and motivation. Leaders who successfully create a culture that values progress acknowledgment understand that this appreciation leads to increased intrinsic motivation. The act of charting progress serves as a visual testament to hard work and dedication, which in turn enhances morale and fosters greater intrinsic engagement.

Effective progress monitoring is tailored to the team and the objectives. While some teams may thrive with quantitative metrics, others might benefit from qualitative observations. It could be a blend of both, depending on the complexity of the goals. The leader's job is to recognize what resonates best with their team, ensuring the monitoring process is insightful and empowering rather than rote and disheartening.

Alongside tracking the hard data of progress, there must be an awareness of the team's emotional landscape as well. Leaders should be attuned to the levels of stress, satisfaction, and fatigue within their teams. Understanding these emotional undercurrents enables the leader to manage workloads and provide support where it's needed, preventing burnout and promoting sustained effort and wellness.

Implementing technological tools can streamline the process of monitoring. Project management software, analytics platforms, and communication tools can offer real-time insights and foster collaboration. Utilizing these resources effectively can minimize the administrative burden of tracking while maximizing focus on action and decision-making.

Moreover, it's about rhythm as much as it is about routine. Establishing a cadence for these monitoring activities—be it weekly, monthly, or quarterly—brings rhythm into the work process. It sets expectations and normalizes the practice of reflection and adjustment, encouraging consistency in both performance and review.

Transparency in progress monitoring is indispensable. It demystifies the process of achieving goals, showing that success is not a sudden leap but the result of ongoing, concerted efforts. When teams have clear visibility of their progress, it fuels a collective striving for excellence and heightens the sense of shared mission.

Furthermore, leaders must recognize that monitoring progress is an act of engagement and inspiration in itself. It should always be linked to recognition. Pointing out progress reinforces positive behaviors and tactics that are working well and encourages continued effort in those areas. Similarly, identifying areas lagging behind is not about assigning blame but rather about collectively finding solutions and learning from challenges.

Above all, the spirit with which progress monitoring is done can define its impact. Approach it with a mindset that focuses on development, support, and continuous improvement. When done thoughtfully, it shifts from being just an administrative task to a strategic lever for boosting team performance and motivation.

Leaders must embody the virtues of patience and persistence. Not every goal is met on the first attempt, and setbacks are as much a part of the process as successes. The key lies in using the insights from monitoring progress to build resilience and equip the team with the fortitude to persist and overcome obstacles, keeping the momentum steady.

In the grand tapestry of leadership and motivation, monitoring progress is the thread that weaves together the intricate patterns of strategy and execution, vision and reality. It's an active, ongoing process that when executed with fineship assures not only that milestones are attained but that the journey there is robust with learning, growth, and shared victories.

Chapter 5:
The Power of Positive Reinforcement

The journey into the heart of inspiring leadership continues as we turn the spotlight onto one of the most uplifting and transformative aspects of leadership – the power of positive reinforcement. Within the realm of motivation, nothing quite echoes the ripples of impact like the timely and genuine recognition of a team's efforts. Imagine, if you will, the transformation that takes place when a leader replaces criticism with commending, naysaying with nurturing. Envision the strengthened resolve of your team as they bask in the light of appreciation, their aspirations igniting, kindling the fires of productivity and dedication. This chapter isn't simply about why affirmations work; it's a deep dive into how you, as a leader, can skillfully waltz with the principles of reinforcement to elevate morale, cultivate loyalty, and most importantly, unlock the latent potential within each of your team members. When the subtle art of positive reinforcement is embraced, leaders find themselves at the helm of not just a team, but a symphony of motivated individuals harmoniously achieving excellence.

The Basics of Reinforcement Theory

Having laid the groundwork for understanding the elements of motivation and leadership in the preceding chapters, we now turn our attention to the potent concept at the core of motivating behaviors: reinforcement theory. This theory is the foundation upon which the edifice of positive reinforcement is constructed, enabling leaders to effectively nurture and shape their team's performance in profound ways.

Reinforcement theory hinges on the basic principle that behavior is a function of its consequences. The implication for leadership is vast; if you understand how to control, manipulate, or otherwise influence the consequences of your team's actions, you can guide their behaviors in beneficial directions. Positive reinforcement, specifically, involves adding a desirable stimulus after a behavior to increase the likelihood of that behavior being repeated.

Understanding reinforcement theory begins with grasping the four types of consequences that can influence behavior. These include positive reinforcement, negative reinforcement, punishment, and extinction. Positive reinforcement, our focus, deals with adding something favorable following a desired behavior, thus encouraging that behavior to recur. This contrasts with negative reinforcement, which involves removing an unpleasant stimulus to encourage behavior, and punishment, which introduces an adverse outcome to discourage behavior. Extinction takes place when no consequence follows a behavior, leading to its decrease over time.

At the heart of reinforcement theory is the concept of operant conditioning, pioneered by B.F. Skinner. This psychological model suggests that behaviors can be changed based on the consequences they produce. It's vital to understand that the timing and consistency of reinforcements are as significant as the reinforcement itself. Immediate and consistent reinforcement can strongly establish behaviors.

One might wonder, what forms can positive reinforcement take within a team? It's not just about monetary rewards or bonuses. Recognition can be an equally powerful reinforcer – a shoutout in a meeting, a heartfelt thank you, or a commendation certificate. The key is that the reinforcement is meaningful to the individual receiving it.

The leader's role is not merely to provide reinforcement, but also to clearly communicate the behaviors that will lead to such positive outcomes. This clarity ensures that team members understand what is expected of them and what they can do to achieve and receive recognition. In this light, setting SMART goals, as discussed in a previous chapter, becomes intertwined with reinforcement theory; when goals are clear, so are the behaviors that will be positively reinforced.

Further refining our understanding of reinforcement, it's essential to recognize that not all reinforcers are created equal. Reinforcers must be tailored to the individual to be effective. What motivates one person may not have the same effect on another. Therefore, you as a leader must discern the preferences and motivators of each team member.

Another critical element of reinforcement theory is the schedule of reinforcement. Various schedules, such as fixed-ratio, variable-ratio, fixed-interval, and variable-interval, can influence how quickly and steadfastly a behavior is adopted. Leaders can leverage these in different scenarios, depending on the goals and the behaviors desired.

It's not enough to randomly dole out praises or rewards. Leaders must be strategic. Reinforcements must be seen as something earned, not given. This ensures that reinforcements retain their power and effectiveness. Your role is to create a system where positive reinforcement is perceived as a natural result of excellent performance, further driving motivation and engagement.

Moreover, it is important for reinforcements to evolve as the team progresses. Continued growth requires evolving challenges and corresponding reinforcements. As a behavior becomes the norm, leaders should look to reinforce behaviors that represent the next level of performance or mastery.

Lastly, reinforcement theory also teaches the importance of consistency. While reinforcement schedules can vary, applying the consequences of behavior consistently ensures that the message is clear. Inconsistent reinforcement can lead to confusion, diminishing the desired behavior rather than strengthening it.

As a leader, practicing reinforcement theory enables you to influence your team positively, to steer them towards excellence with a gentle, guiding hand rather than imposing authority. Through thoughtful application of reinforcements, you can create an environment where each member feels valued and driven to contribute their best.

Incorporating reinforcement theory into your leadership approach sets the stage for the next sections, where we'll explore how to recognize and reward your team effectively, ensuring that positive reinforcements translate to peak performance and a thriving, motivated team.

Embracing the delicate art and science of reinforcement theory, you equip yourself with the tools to not only enhance the performance of your team but also to instill a lasting sense of empowerment, satisfaction, and commitment to excellence that will resonate throughout your leadership journey.

Understanding the nuances of reinforcement theory is just the beginning. Applying it consistently and thoughtfully will transform your approach to leadership, enable you to harness the true potential of your team, and leave a lasting impression that extends far beyond mere productivity. Your leadership can inspire a legacy of motivation, growth, and positive change.

Recognizing and Rewarding Your Team Effectively

As leaders, diving into the nitty-gritty of motivating our teams, we must acknowledge the transformative power of recognizing and rewarding our team members effectively. This act not just acknowledges good work but also stimulates the quest for excellence across the board. Recognition, at its core, is a fundamental human need, and rewarding a job well done encourages productivity and reinforces the behaviors that drive a team towards success.

Effective recognition and reward are not one-size-fits-all; they're as diverse as your team members themselves. A handwritten note of thanks, a public acknowledgment during a meeting, or a thoughtful gift can mean more than a generic certificate of appreciation. It's crucial to find out what makes each team member tick to offer a reward that truly resonates.

Timing plays a pivotal role in recognition. Immediate praise following an achievement has a stronger impact than delayed acknowledgment. Seizing the moment to celebrate your team's victories instills a sense of immediacy and importance to their contributions and fosters an environment where positive feedback is anticipated and valued.

It's not just about big achievements either. Recognizing the small steps towards a larger goal inspires continued effort and demonstrates that no contribution is too small to be valued. Every piece of the puzzle is crucial, and each member's work, no matter how minute it may seem, is essential to the overall success of the project. This is crucial for sustained motivation.

Personalization is key when it comes to rewarding your team. Explore creative reward options – maybe an extra day off for someone who values time with family or recognition in front of peers for someone who appreciates public acclaim. The more tailored the reward, the more meaningful it becomes. Thus, understanding your team's individual preferences is an ongoing leadership task.

However, the act of recognition should not just be left to the leader. Encouraging peer-to-peer recognition creates a culture of appreciation that permeates throughout the team. A simple peer-nominated award during meetings can be an empowering tool. It not only acknowledges good work but also strengthens team bonds.

Recognition should always be tied to clearly defined goals and values. This alignment ensures that the behaviors being rewarded are those that align with the team's purpose and the organization's culture. It's a way to communicate, "This is what excellence looks like within our context."

Moreover, transparency in recognizing and rewarding efforts is imperative. Publicly setting benchmarks for recognition lets team members know what they are working towards and allows them to see that the process is fair and open. Everyone should know the "why" and "how" behind the recognition, which builds trust in the leader and the system.

Non-material rewards can be just as, if not more, effective than material ones. Opportunities for growth, such as leading a new project, attending a professional conference, or participating in advanced training, are valuable ways to recognize someone's potential and fuel their professional journey. These experiences can be transformative, offering long-term benefits to the individual and the team.

Balancing rewards to reflect both individual and team accomplishments is essential. While individuals love to be recognized, team rewards foster a sense of collective achievement and unity. Group celebrations or rewards ensure that the team's collaborative effort is celebrated, and not just the stars among them.

In a similar vein, not all recognition should come from above. Creating systems where team members can recognize one another fosters a supportive atmosphere. This lateral appreciation helps in building interdependence and trust among team members.

Recognition can also be coupled with reflection. Teams that take the time to reflect on their successes and the behaviors that led to them are more likely to repeat those actions. This reflection can be facilitated during debriefing sessions post a project's completion or during performance reviews.

Lastly, recognition should evolve as the team does. As ambitions grow and targets change, so too should the way recognition and rewards are approached. It's essential for leaders to stay attuned to their team's developing needs and adapt recognition strategies accordingly.

In conclusion, recognizing and rewarding your team effectively isn't a mere supplementary task; it's an intrinsic part of nurturing your team's work ethic, cooperation, and loyalty. The emotional and psychological boost that comes from feeling valued cannot be overstated. It translates into higher levels of engagement, productivity, and an invigorating work culture that attracts and retains top talent.

Stepping into the next chapters of our quest to inspire, motivate, and lead, always carry with you the understanding that the art of recognizing and rewarding effectively is essential to galvanizing your team to achieve new heights. Championing this can ultimately shape not just the future of your team, but also the destiny of the entire organization.

Chapter 6:
Overcoming Obstacles to Motivation

As leaders journey deeper into the intricacies of motivating their teams, it becomes evident that they must also become adept at navigating the labyrinth of challenges that can impede motivation. Whether it's the specter of burnout looming over your team or the subtle onset of complacency, these obstacles are not insurmountable. It's paramount for leaders to cultivate an environment where resilience acts as the bedrock upon which motivation can thrive, even in the face of adversity. It's about evolving beyond short-term fixes and cultivating a sustained drive that withstands the ebb and flow of workplace dynamics. Leaders must recognize that motivation is not just about the highs but also about managing the lows effectively. This includes engaging in honest self-reflection, resiliently adapting strategies, and infusing the workplace with an energy that converts challenges into opportunities for growth. Such perseverance doesn't just build motivation; it transforms teams into dynamos of inspiration and productivity, shaping them into more than the sum of their parts.

Identifying and Addressing Burnout

Burnout is a formidable obstacle to motivation and is an issue that can quietly infiltrate the ranks of a team, undermining the passion and drive that once animated its members. As a leader, recognizing the signs of burnout in your team—and within yourself—is essential to preserving the collective ambition and well-being of your group.

Burnout often manifests as a reduction in performance, a lack of enthusiasm, signs of detachment, and a general sense of exhaustion. These symptoms stem from prolonged periods of stress or frustration, frequently without adequate relief or reward. Leaders who identify these signs early can take proactive steps to address the underlying causes and prevent the full onset of burnout.

It's not enough to merely spot the warning signs; we must also understand the factors contributing to burnout. Are workloads too heavy? Is there a lack of control or autonomy in the way tasks are managed? Perhaps the team's efforts are not being recognized, or they feel that their work lacks meaning. Each of these factors alone, and especially in combination, can lead to burnout.

Open communication is an essential tool in combating burnout. Create safe spaces for your team members to express their concerns and struggles. These conversations can offer insights into what's affecting their emotional and mental health, laying the groundwork for effective solutions.

A leader's ability to facilitate a healthy work-life balance cannot be overstressed. Encouraging your team to take regular breaks, use their vacation time, and cultivate interests outside of work can restore their energy and perspective. Your example in maintaining your own balance will speak volumes about the value you place on well-being.

Redistributing workload may also be required to address burnout. Balanced workloads ensure no team member is overwhelmed, and it promotes efficiency. This may involve streamlining processes, identifying areas of waste, or bringing in additional resources or support.

Professional development opportunities can reinvigorate a team member's sense of purpose and spark new interest in their work.

Offering training and developmental tasks allows your team to grow their skills, keeping their work fresh and engaging.

Normalize rest and recovery as integral to high performance, just as athletes must rest between games to perform at their best. Structure projects with phases of intense work followed by periods of recovery, and ensure your team understands that rest isn't a reward for hard work—it's a prerequisite.

When all else fails, it might be necessary to encourage a team member to take a step back. In extreme cases, a sabbatical or a temporary change of projects may help to reset their motivation and recharge their batteries. While it may be a short-term loss for the team, the long-term benefits of rejuvenated vigor can far outweigh the temporary gap.

Acknowledge your own susceptibility to burnout and demonstrate self-awareness. As a leader, if you're running on empty, your team will likely follow suit. Invest in your self-care and be a model for sustainable work practices.

Recognition can act as a powerful antidote to feelings of futility. Regularly acknowledging the hard work and successes of your team, both publicly and privately, can breathe life back into their sails and rekindle their intrinsic motivation.

Ultimately, the key to addressing burnout lies in fostering an environment where well-being is woven into the fabric of the workplace culture. This includes encouraging healthy physical routines, mental health days, and creating a community of support within the team.

Burnout doesn't dissipate on its own and requires intentional action. A leader's thoughtful and caring approach to prevention and intervention can sustain a team's motivation. Encourage open dialogues where team members can voice their limits and help them find joy and purpose in their roles once again.

Through vigilance and compassionate leadership, burnout can be confronted and vanquished, allowing motivation to flourish anew. By investing in the holistic well-being of your team, you lay the groundwork for a resilient, engaged, and enthusiastic group. Remember, a motivated team is an unstoppable force, and preventing burnout keeps the path to success brightly lit.

As a last thought on this complex challenge, remember the power of small gestures and the profound impact they can have on an individual's sense of value and morale. A coffee catch-up, an unexpected note of appreciation, or a simple 'Thank you for your hard work' can sometimes make all the difference, rekindling the flame of motivation in the heart of a team member close to burning out.

Creating Resilience in Your Team

In the landscape of modern leadership, the most successful teams are the ones that can weather the storms of uncertainty and persist in the face of challenges. This resilience is not intrinsic; it is built through deliberate action and the cultivation of a supportive environment. A leader's role is pivotal in fostering this tenacity within their team, transforming obstacles into opportunities for growth and innovation.

To create resilience, you must first understand its essence — it is the capacity to recover quickly from difficulties, the mental reservoir of strength that teams draw upon in times of stress. As a leader, imparting this quality to your team begins with a foundation of trust. Trust allows team members to take risks and face challenges, knowing they have the support of the group and its leader.

Communication is your ally in building resilience. This means not just delivering information, but also encouraging an open dialogue where concerns and fears can be expressed without judgment. By cultivating an environment where team members feel heard and valued, you reinforce their sense of belonging and shared purpose.

Resilience is also strengthened by embracing a mindset that views failure not as a defeat, but as a vital part of the learning process. Encourage your team to push boundaries and innovate, reassuring them that setbacks are natural and provide valuable insight. When members are not paralyzed by the fear of failure, they are more willing to attempt novel solutions to problems.

Diversity of thought and experience is a boon to resilience. When team members come from various backgrounds, they bring unique perspectives that can help the team to navigate through challenges more effectively. Promoting inclusivity not only broadens the team's outlook but also supports a culture where every contribution is valued.

Preparation and ongoing development are key components of resilience. Invest in training that equips your team members with not just technical skills, but also with strategies to manage stress, resolve conflict, and recover from setbacks. When team members are better prepared, they are more likely to face adversity with confidence.

Emphasize the importance of self-care and work-life balance. Resilient teams are composed of individuals who are physically and mentally healthy. Encourage team members to care for themselves outside of work so that they can bring their best selves to the tasks at hand.

Mindset is everything. Foster a growth mindset within your team that emphasizes effort and progress over perfection. This type of mindset empowers your team to strive for continuous improvement rather than being bogged down by the need to achieve immediate perfection.

Transparent leadership is indispensable when fortifying resilience. When team members see their leaders face challenges head-on, admit to mistakes, and stay true to their values, they feel empowered to duplicate these behaviors. This leads to a team that is less afraid of encountering hurdles and more equipped to deal with them when they arise.

Goals are not just destinations but also tools for building resilience. Set challenging yet attainable goals and celebrate the milestones along the way. This not only propels progress but also builds the muscle of perseverance as the team works through challenges towards achieving these goals.

Resilience doesn't mean going it alone. Encourage collaboration and the sharing of workload. When team members pull together and support one another, they learn that they are not isolated in facing difficulties, bolstering the team's collective strength.

Feedback is a two-way street instrumental in creating a resilient team. Establish modes for constructive feedback that enable members to reflect on and learn from experiences. This continuous flow of feedback helps the team to adapt and refine strategies, reinforcing resilience to future challenges.

A culture of appreciation goes a long way. Recognize and reward resilience just as you would other accomplishments. Highlighting instances where the team or individuals have bounced back or adapted can serve as motivation for others and set the standard for expected behavior.

Leverage adversity as a team bonding experience. When your team overcomes challenges together, it builds a shared narrative of strength and the ability for collective problem-solving. Encourage team members to share their stories of resilience and learn from one another, fostering a sense of unity and camaraderie.

Finally, model resilience yourself. As a leader, your team looks to you for cues on how to react in the face of adversity. If you maintain a positive and determined outlook, your team is likely to mirror this attitude. Demonstrate through your own actions how challenges can be met with grace and resolve, and your team will follow suit.

Creating resilience in your team is a vital endeavor that pays off in the form of increased adaptability, innovation, and sustained motivation. As teams face inevitable challenges, it is the resilient ones that stand tall and not only survive but thrive. It is your privilege and responsibility as a leader to nurture and encourage this invaluable trait within your team.

Chapter 7:
The Impact of Organizational Culture

As we turn the page on overcoming motivational obstacles, let's delve into the heart of organizational culture and its profound influence on every individual within your team. Any seasoned leader knows that the values, expectations, and practices that permeate an organization do more than just fill an employee handbook; they breathe life into the day-to-day experiences and can elevate motivation or stifle it. Recognizing that a team's environment acts as the soil from which success either flourishes or withers is crucial. Leaders who cultivate a culture resonating with trust, support, flexibility, and recognition not only unlock the latent potential within their teams but also create ripples that echo through productivity, innovation, and, ultimately, an organization's legacy. Such a culture amplifies each team member's intrinsic motivation and aligns it with the company's mission, encouraging a synergetic workplace where individuals don't just work—they thrive.

Shaping a Motivational Work Environment

As we delve deeper into the critical role of organizational culture, it's essential to understand how to create a work environment that breathes motivation into every corner. A motivated workforce can achieve the unimaginable, propelling a company towards success with both energy and commitment. Leaders play a pivotal role in sculpting such an environment; it begins with recognizing the profound impact a thoughtfully cultivated workspace can have on the spirit and productivity of a team.

Consider the atmosphere that greets someone the moment they step through the doors of your organization. Is it one of excitement, possibility, and recognition? The tone is set from that initial moment and reverberates through every interaction and task. Establishing a motivational setting isn't just an ideal to strive for; it's a strategic move that can define the trajectory of your company's growth and the satisfaction of your team members.

It starts with the physical workspace. Leaders are often surprised at the enormous difference that a well-designed, comfortable, and stimulating environment can make. Invest in spaces that inspire collaboration and creativity. Think about adaptable areas where teams can gather informally, brainstorms without barriers, and maintain comfort throughout long projects. Natural light, plants, and artwork can transform the mundane into the dynamic. But it goes beyond the tangibles. The ambience, the energy, and the message your space sends can't be underestimated. It needs to say, 'Here, you matter, and your ideas can flourish.'

Empathy and understanding form the cornerstone of a motivational work environment. Leaders must actively engage in the aspirations and challenges of their team, acting as both a guide and a supporter. By genuinely caring about each individual's motives and well-being, leaders can foster a nurturing atmosphere where everyone feels valued and understood. It's this personalized approach that can make a team member go above and beyond, not because they have to, but because they want to contribute to a culture that respects and appreciates them.

Communication within this environment is less about dictating and more about dialogue. Encourage open discussions, invite a free exchange of ideas, and demonstrate that every voice holds weight.

When team members know their opinions are not only heard but also can effect change, they're more engaged and invested in the outcomes.

One powerful method to motivate is through collective goal setting. When teams set goals together, a shared purpose emerges, forging a stronger bond between members. Ensuring that these goals align with personal aspirations creates a win-win situation. Each achievement adds to the sense of team triumph and personal satisfaction, infusing the workplace with renewed vigor.

Recognizing and celebrating achievements is just as crucial as setting goals. Acknowledge efforts, spotlight successes, and share these stories across the company. This recognition doesn't always need to be grand gestures; sometimes, a heartfelt thank-you or a handwritten note can be incredibly impactful. This positive reinforcement builds an environment where people not only feel seen but also understand that their contributions are essential to the collective success.

Bearing in mind the diversity of what motivates individuals is key. Flexibility in understanding personal drivers allows leaders to tailor their approach to each member of their team. Some may find motivation in public recognition, while others may be driven by challenging projects or opportunities for professional growth. This tailored approach speaks volumes to your team, showing them that their unique qualities are both recognized and valued.

In this nurturing space, don't neglect the role of professional development. A motivational work environment is one where growth is not only possible—it's expected and supported. Offer training, mentorship, and avenues for advancement. When team members see that their career progression is a priority for the organization, their alignment with the company's vision strengthens, as does their drive to contribute to its success.

Transparency and trust are the bedrocks of a motivational culture. Cultivate an environment where honesty is the norm, where team members can rely on clear expectations and constructive feedback. When trust permeates the team, it creates a strong and secure foundation from which individuals can operate with confidence and autonomy.

It's also necessary to address the inevitable setbacks with a constructive mindset. A resilient work environment is one that sees failure as a necessary catalyst for innovation and learning. When leaders approach challenges as opportunities for growth, team members feel empowered and less apprehensive about taking calculated risks.

Finally, do not underestimate the impact of leading by example. Leaders who consistently demonstrate their commitment, who are the first to roll up their sleeves when needed, and who maintain a positive outlook set the pace for the entire team. Your own energy and passion are contagious, and they can kindle the same in the people you lead.

Constructing a motivational work environment doesn't happen overnight, and it isn't a static achievement. It's an ongoing effort, a pulse that must be regularly checked and revitalized. It demands attentiveness to the evolving needs of your team and the agility to adapt. Revisit policies, practices, and the physical environment to ensure they continue to align with the aim of motivating and supporting your team.

As a leaders, you have the power to shape the daily experience of your team members. By fostering an inclusive, supportive, and stimulating work environment, you not only accelerate their success and satisfaction but also the forward momentum of your organization. The ripples of a motivational culture are far-reaching, beyond the individual, through the organization, and into the broader community.

In summary, shaping a motivational work environment is an art and a science. It draws on aesthetics, empathy, strategy, and personal connection. It requires a visionary approach that can unite a diverse team's individual motivations with the organization's overarching goals. Arm yourself with the belief that you can craft this environment, and you'll be well on your way to nurturing a workplace where motivation flourishes and people feel inspired to achieve greatness.

Leading by Example: Modeling Desired Behaviors

When you consider the vast impact organizational culture has on a team's dynamics, it's evident that as a leader, you play a pivotal role in shaping that culture through your actions and behaviors. Your team looks to you not only for direction but also for inspiration and guidance. This is where the principle of leading by example becomes your strongest asset. By modeling the desired behaviors, you create a living blueprint for your team to follow.

Consider your values and principles as the foundation on which your organization's culture is built. These aren't merely words on a page but rather a set of actionable practices that you embody every single day. If you seek a culture of integrity, it starts with you being honest in your dealings and transparent in your communication. Similarly, if innovation is the goal, the willingness to embrace risk and learn from failure should be evident in your leadership approach.

Modeling desired behaviors is about consistency. It's not enough to demonstrate the right behaviors sporadically; it requires a steady commitment that your team can depend on. This consistency builds trust – the element most critical to the efficacy of your leadership. When your team trusts you, they are more likely to take risks, be honest with you, and follow your lead. Every action you take either builds or erodes this trust.

Your ability to maintain composure under pressure isn't just a personal skill; it sends a message to your team about resilience and determination. The manner in which you tackle challenges serves as an implicit guide for your teammates when they face their own obstacles. By maintaining a calm and strategic approach, you set the tone for the team's response to adversity.

Communication is another area where leading by example is essential. Just as you encourage your team to be clear and articulate, your communication should exemplify these traits. Listening is just as important as speaking. If your team sees you actively listening to understand and not just to respond, they are likely to mirror this valuable behavior, leading to better understanding and collaboration within the group.

Respect and inclusivity are also behaviors that resonate deeply when led by example. A culture that values every team member regardless of their role or background is not a happenstance. It reflects your own practice of giving everyone a voice and showing appreciation for diverse perspectives. This practice lays down the groundwork for a culture where every individual feels valued and heard.

Delegation also speaks volumes about trust. By empowering your team with responsibilities, you signal your confidence in their capabilities, which, in turn, boosts their confidence and fosters ownership of their roles. If you micromanage, you might inadvertently suggest that you don't trust your team's abilities, which can stifle initiative and motivation.

Giving feedback effectively is a key part of leadership. When providing constructive criticism, do so in a manner that is supportive and aimed at growth. Celebrate the wins just as openly. Your approach to feedback teaches your team how to interact with each other and reinforces the idea that growth is a shared journey.

Another crucial behavior to model is learning from mistakes. Rather than hide your errors, acknowledge them and use them as teaching moments. This creates an environment where it's safe to take measured risks and where continual learning is valued over perfection. This openness can instill a powerful motivation to innovate and improve.

Work-life balance is an often-discussed but rarely well-modeled aspect of work culture. If you preach the importance of downtime but regularly send emails late at night, weekends, or while on vacation, you imply an expectation that your team should do the same. Instead, by genuinely disconnecting when needed, you show that you prioritize well-being alongside productivity.

Empathy and care for your team should not be overlooked. These are behaviors that, when demonstrated, can deeply enhance the relational dynamics within your team. If you show that you're attentive to the needs and concerns of your team members, they, too, will cultivate this sensitivity, creating a culture of support and collaboration.

In a world that is constantly evolving, adaptability becomes a key trait for success. Your willingness to embrace change and approach new ideas with enthusiasm models a proactive, rather than reactive, approach to the future. This can encourage your team members to embrace innovation and remain flexible, which is crucial for growth and sustainability.

Finally, integrity should be the thread that ties all these behaviors together. Modeling ethical behavior, honoring commitments, and treating everyone with respect regardless of the circumstance sets a powerful example for the team to emulate. It cements a culture where ethical behavior is the norm, not the exception.

In conclusion, remember that cultural transformation begins with you. Each behavior you exhibit is like a pebble thrown into a pond, creating ripples that spread across your team. By consciously modeling desired behaviors, you not only set the standard but also harness the influence of your position to inspire and bring out the best in those around you. This alignment of personal practice with professional expectations is a true mark of leadership excellence.

Keep in mind that effective leadership is not about perfection but progress. As you strive to model these behaviors, be patient with yourself and maintain an openness to growth. Your journey will inevitably influence the journey of your entire team, creating an organizational culture that thrives on motivation, collaboration, and shared success.

Chapter 8:
Inspiring Through Vision and Purpose

Having woven the robust fabric of motivation and potent organizational culture, let's now illuminate the path to harness the compelling force of vision and purpose. A leader's call echoes beyond the mundane tasks, it reaches into the realm of what could be, where aspirations shape reality and where every member finds their beat in the rhythmic march towards a common goal. Imagine the power of a clearly articulated vision, a lighthouse guiding your team through the fog of daily operations, where each step is purpose-driven and every effort is a brick in the fortress of your collective dreams. It's this allure, this gravitational pull of a worthy pursuit that binds individuals together, turning cogs into comrades battling for a future they each own a stake in. As your team's compass, you must paint a future so vivid, so enticing, that the path to excellence becomes not just traveled but cherished. For in the hearts of those who share your vision lies an unstoppable force, an army fueled not just by the promise of success but by the noble pursuit of something greater than themselves. This chapter isn't just about setting a direction; it's about kindling a fire within, uniting your team under the banner of a shared destiny, and creating a legacy punctuated by the milestones of collective triumph.

Crafting and Communicating Your Vision

Vision drives progress. It is the beacon that guides and aligns effort, kindles inspiration, and gives purpose to every action within a team. Executed effectively, a vision becomes more than a statement; it becomes the heartbeat of an organization, fueling the passion and innovation that transforms workplaces and the world.

To craft a vision that resonates, you'll need to delve deep into the core of your values and the ultimate impact you wish to create. A well-constructed vision does not simply detail the work to be done but instead paints an image of the world changed by that work. Begin with your 'why' – the reason that ignites your drive and encapsulates the significance of the journey you're inviting others to join.

Once your 'why' is in focus, distill it into a clear, compelling vision statement. Clarity is the beacon that cuts through fog; thus, your vision must not languish in ambiguity. It should evoke emotion and spark a connection that reaches beyond logic, into the realm where deep-seated aspirations lie. The more poignant and vivid your visualization, the stronger it will resonate with others, pulling them into a shared future with enthusiasm and commitment.

But crafting a striking vision isn't the end destination; it's merely the beginning. Communication breathes life into your vision. It's not enough to display your vision statement on walls or recite it in meetings; you need to weave it into the fabric of everyday conversations, decision-making, and the narratives that encompass your leadership.

When communicating your vision, embody it. Let your actions articulate the commitment to the destination you've charted. People follow what they see more readily than what they hear, so show them what living the vision looks like. You are the primary ambassador of the future you've envisioned, after all, and your consistent example sets the standard for others to follow.

Engage in storytelling to bring your vision to life. Stories captivate and convey meaning in ways that facts and figures never could. Share tales of success that exemplify the vision in action, or paint scenarios that frame the future in tangible terms. Through storytelling, the abstract becomes relatable, and the distant horizon seems that much closer.

Listening is also an essential part of communication. As much as you share the vision, you must also create spaces for dialogue around it. Encourage others to share their interpretations and how they see their role in this collective journey. Such conversations not only reinforce the vision but can also offer fresh perspectives that enrich its realization.

Recognize that the process of internalizing a vision doesn't happen overnight. It requires reinforcement, which is why your vision must not only be communicated once but continuously—and in various ways. Use regular team meetings, one-on-ones, company-wide updates, email newsletters, and informal social interactions as platforms to reinforce the vision.

As time progresses and your team or organization evolves, revisit and, if necessary, refine your vision. A vision that adapts to new challenges, opportunities, and insights retains its relevance and rallying power. Never forget that a static vision can fast become obsolete in a dynamic environment.

Empower your team by linking their contributions to the vision's success. When individuals understand how their roles fit into the larger picture, motivation and accountability soar. A person who sees their work as instrumental to achieving the vision is infinitely more engaged and driven.

Train and mentor future leaders to understand and communicate the vision just as passionately as you do. Building a cadre of vision ambassadors amplifies the reach and strength of your message and ensures that the vision thrives beyond your direct influence.

Be patient, yet persistent. Cultivating a shared vision within the soul of an organization is no small feat; it takes time and tenacity. With every discussion, decision, and directive, you are sewing seeds. Some may take root quickly, others may need more nurturing, but each is critical to the eventual blossoming of the future you envision.

Crafting and communicating your vision is a journey that commands both strategic thought and heartfelt authenticity. When the head and the heart align, the power of a vision can become the most profound tool for inspiration and purpose in a leader's arsenal. Embrace this journey, and let your vision illuminate the path to collective achievement and growth.

Remember, a leader's vision acts as a compass in times of uncertainty and a rally cry in moments of challenge. It encourages resilience and fosters an environment where innovation thrives. By embodying your vision, consistently communicating it, and fostering ownership among your team, you harness the collective power of shared purpose.

Your leadership journey is as unique as the vision you craft, but the principles of creating and communicating it are universally potent. With an authentic, vivid, and actively shared vision, you don't just lead a team—you lead a movement. And movements have the power to change the world. So, set your sights on the horizon and lead boldly towards it. Your team is ready to follow.

Connecting Individual Roles to the Bigger Picture

Leadership is often described as a journey of making an array of disparate parts come together in harmony toward a shared objective. While crafting and communicating a compelling vision provides direction, it's the nuanced art of connecting individual roles to that vision that truly inspires teams to align their daily work with the larger goals of the organization. When each team member recognizes how their efforts fit into the bigger picture, their sense of purpose intensifies, and their commitment to the shared mission solidifies.

Imagine the intricate workings of a clock. Each cog, wheel, and spring has a specific function that contributes to the clock's ability to keep time. Similarly, in any organization, every role – no matter how seemingly small – is essential to the achievement of the whole. To instill this understanding, leaders should start by clearly defining how each role intersects with the company's objectives. This acts as a catalyst for employees to see the value in what they do and can transform even the most routine tasks into meaningful contributions.

Communication is a key component in this process. Without clear, continuous discussion about goals, values, and how each task moves the needle, employees may feel disconnected. Therefore, it's important to consistently articulate the ways in which specific roles and projects help the organization to advance. This can be fulfilled through regular team meetings, one-on-one sessions, and company-wide communications that highlight individual and group contributions to the company's objectives.

Recognizing individual efforts and linking them to the success of larger projects can also be a powerful motivational tool. When people know that their work is noticed and valued, they are more likely to take initiative and go above and beyond. Acknowledging the role they play in the success of the organization helps foster a sense of ownership and pride in their work.

As leaders, it's imperative to help team members visualize the end result of their work. Setting short-term, tangible milestones that connect to the long-term vision can help individuals visualize their impact. These milestones offer a clear sense of progress and achievement that is directly connected to the bigger picture, making the vision a reality one step at a time.

Involving team members in strategic planning sessions can further imbue them with the sense that they are an integral part of the company's future. In these discussions, invite feedback and insights on how to better align individual efforts with the overall goals. Teams that feel they have a say in the direction of their work are more invested in the outcome.

A leader must also be a mentor and a coach, guiding employees through challenges and encouraging them to grow within their roles. This guidance should always tie back to how their personal growth benefits not just themselves but also the organizational mission. It's a reciprocal relationship where individual advancement and organizational success fuel each other.

It's important to recognize that not all contributions are easily quantifiable, yet they are just as crucial. Some team members might be fostering the collaborative culture or providing the unwavering support that others rely on. Highlight how these immeasurable contributions also play a key role in achieving the vision, as they often form the social glue that holds the team together.

Storytelling can be a powerful method to illustrate the importance of individual roles within the bigger picture. Share stories of how different roles have made significant impacts on the organization's journey. These narratives not only celebrate achievements but also demonstrate, in a vivid and relatable manner, how each person is part of a larger story.

Cross-functional alignment is also crucial. Encourage collaboration across departments so all employees understand how their roles intersect and support one another. This can lead to improved communication, innovation, and a unified approach to problem-solving, all while reinforcing the interconnected nature of individual efforts.

When setting objectives, utilize a participative goal-setting process. Allow employees to set their personal goals in alignment with the company's ambitions. This gives them autonomy to own their goals and understand how achieving them contributes to the broader objectives, thereby making the linkage to the bigger picture a personal commitment rather than a top-down directive.

Diversity of thought and perspective is an asset to be leveraged when aligning individual roles to the greater vision. Encourage team members from different backgrounds and experiences to provide insights into how their unique perspectives and skills can serve the broader objectives. This not only promotes inclusion but also enriches the implementation of the vision.

Maintain transparency about the state of the company and its performance. When individuals understand how their efforts are contributing to the organization's overall health, they can better appreciate their role in its success or what needs to be addressed in times of challenge. This openness builds trust and promotes a culture of shared responsibility.

Don't forget the power of reflection. Regularly reflecting on what has been achieved and what's ahead is instrumental. During these reflective moments, revisit individual contributions and reemphasize their link to wider organizational achievements. Encourage your team to recognize not only what they have accomplished but also the collective progress made possible through their individual roles.

In the grand tapestry of organizational success, each thread – each role – is vital. The leader's task is to illuminate how these threads interweave to create the rich, vibrant picture of the company's vision. It's this understanding that transforms ordinary tasks into extraordinary purpose, galvanizing individuals into a unified force capable of achieving great things. By connecting individual roles to the bigger picture, a leader not only inspires but also empowers each team member to contribute to a story much larger than themselves.

Chapter 9:
Developing and Leading Teams

To forge a team that not only meets expectations but surpasses them, a leader must understand the delicate art of balance—between the needs of the individual and the requirements of the team, between the vision of success and the steps to reach it. In this chapter, we'll explore the evolutionary stages of team development and unearth strategies to guide you through each phase, ensuring your stewardship leads to a synergy that resonates with collaboration and collective success. The true test of leadership lies in the crucible of team dynamics, where a leader's task is to sculpt an atmosphere of trust, open communication, and unified purpose. It's about nurturing each member's potential while cementing a shared identity that empowers and propels the team towards excellence. So let's venture into the craft of cultivating teams that are resilient, innovative, and reflective of the collective strength found in their diversity of thought, experience, and perspectives.

Stages of Team Development

Embarking on the journey of team formation and evolution can be compared to navigating the unknown waters of leadership. Understanding the stages through which a team progresses is crucial for any leader aiming to cultivate a high-performing and cohesive unit. The pathway your team traverses is not a straight line but a series of gates, each opening to a new landscapes of challenges and triumphs.

The initial phase of team development is **Forming**. During this stage, team members are introduced, often treading lightly, as they scope out the social terrain. It's a time of polite interactions, of people trying to understand their place within the team and the expectations that come with it. You, as a leader, must guide your team through this stage with a welcoming and affirming hand, setting clear objectives and making roles known to everyone. Knitting bonds early on sets a solid foundation for what is to come.

As footsteps become firmer, teams enter the **Storming** phase. Here, the novelty of new relationships has worn off, and the differing opinions and clashing personalities ascend like the inevitable storms they are named for. This stage tests team cohesion and demands a leader's attention to conflict resolution. It's your role to navigate these rough seas with a steady hand, fostering open communication and helping team members focus on common goals rather than personal disputes.

Passing through the storm, teams emerge into the phase of **Norming**. With conflicts largely settled and hierarchies established, the group starts to operate with greater harmony. An atmosphere of mutual respect and understanding develops as routines are formed, and team members learn to work with one another's strengths and weaknesses. Here, you as the leader can encourage the development of team norms that align with organizational values and goals. It's a time for consolidation and strengthening unity.

Further along the developmental road lies the **Performing** stage. Teams at this level are characterized by their high efficiency, autonomy, and ability to handle complex tasks with minimal supervision. Like a well-tuned orchestra, each member plays their part perfectly, supporting one another in a symphony of productivity. Here, your role transitions from direct oversight to empowerment as your team members take more ownership of their work.

Some teams eventually encounter the often-overlooked stage of **Adjourning**, also known as *Mourning*. This is particularly relevant for project-based teams that disband once their objectives are met. This stage can provoke a range of emotions, from pride to sadness, as members prepare to move on. Celebrating the team's successes and acknowledging the journey is essential in providing closure and helping members transition with a sense of accomplishment.

To lead effectively through these stages, it's imperative that you comprehend that each brings distinctive motivational needs. During Forming, an aura of curiosity and anticipation means that motivation will naturally spring from the excitement of new beginnings. Offering support, providing clear structure, and aligning your team with a compelling purpose infuse motivation into their veins.

In the Storming stage, frustration might divert your team's energy from productive tasks to internecine skirmishes. It's your task to channel this energy back into motivation by emphasizing individual strengths, resolving conflicts positively, and keeping the team's eyes on their shared objectives.

Throughout Norming, motivation stems from developing competence and cohesion. Recognize milestones and the evolving dynamics of your team. Foster a culture of appreciation and highlight how collective efforts are moving the needle closer to your collective aspirations.

When your team hits the Performing stage, motivation becomes intrinsic as the satisfaction of well-executed work fuels their drive. At this stage, your role in sustaining motivation is less about driving it and more about maintaining an environment where it can thrive independently. Ensure that there are opportunities for growth and that you entrust your team with the sense that they are steering the ship as much as you are.

The Adjourning stage requires a careful approach to motivation. It involves shifting focus from collective achievements to individual next steps. Acknowledge each member's contributions and facilitate opportunities for reflection. This can transform the ending of one team's journey into the motivational launchpad for future endeavors.

With these stages in mind, remember that no two teams are alike, and they may progress at varying paces, sometimes looping back to previous stages or skipping stages entirely. Your awareness and adaptability as a leader are keys to guiding them through this nonlinear progression.

Moreover, conflicts, while often viewed negatively, can serve as opportunities for growth when managed well. In the storming phase, drawing out the best in each team member can transform a potential breakdown into a breakthrough, setting the scene for deeper trust and camaraderie.

When reaching the Norming and Performing stages, establishing rituals and traditions can create a sense of belonging that sustains motivation. Perhaps a weekly team huddle to share successes, or a monthly 'innovation day' when team members can work on pet projects. These moments serve to remind everyone that, beyond tasks and deadlines, there's a team spirit that prevails.

In guiding teams, it is beneficial to recognize that their evolution is comparable to a narrative arc, with each stage presenting its plot, challenges, and character development. As a leader, you are both author and audience, shaping the story while appreciating the unique contributions of each character – your team members.

Ultimately, an understanding of the developmental stages of a team provides you with the blueprint to tailor your leadership strategies. By appreciating the mechanics behind team dynamics, you can engineer an environment conducive to motivation, collaboration, and outstanding performance. It's not just about getting your team from point A to B; it's about how they grow, together and individually, during the journey.

This nuanced understanding of group behavior will not only enhance your leadership arsenal but also transform the way you perceive the unfolding drama of team development. As a result, you're not just a leader; you are a cultivator of talent, a navigator of complexities, and a beacon of inspiration for teams embarking on the adventure of achievement. Recognize that the true art of leadership lies not in marching your team across the finish line but in orchestrating a journey that leaves every member empowered, enriched, and eager for the next challenge.

Facilitating Collaboration and Team Synergy

In the journey of developing and leading teams, the crib stone beneath the arch of success is facilitating collaboration and team synergy. Collaboration is the heartbeat of a robust team, pumping vibrancy and life into projects and aspirations. As a leader, fostering an environment where collaborative sparks fly and team synergy thrives isn't just beneficial; it is essential.

Team synergy occurs when the collective output of a group surpasses the sum of individual contributions. To reach this pinnacle, you must nurture a culture of openness and trust. Begin by creating safe spaces for dialogue - environments where every team member feels valued and heard. This foundation sets the stage for a synergy that transcends mere cooperation.

Cultivating collaboration requires dismantling silos and encouraging cross-functional engagement. Initiate forums and workshops that bring diverse skill sets together, blending them like colours on a palette to create new hues of innovation. This not only enriches the project at hand but also bolsters individual growth as team members learn from each other's perspectives and expertise.

Effective collaboration also hinges on clear, congruent goals. When each team member understands the vision and their role within it, a powerful alignment takes root. This clarity, like a compass, guides collaborative efforts in a focused direction, preventing the drift that often occurs in teams lacking unified purpose.

Communication is the lifeline of teamwork, and as a leader, mastering the art of facilitating productive conversations is key. Embrace techniques that stimulate active engagement, like brainstorming sessions and regular team huddles, to foster an exchange of ideas. Encouraging dialogues keeps the team's collective mind mapping pathways to success.

Balance in team dynamics is paramount. Recognizing the unique strengths of each member and positioning them accordingly can unleash a dynamic force. This strategic placement, akin to an orchestra conductor ensuring each instrument is at the right pitch, maximizes the team's harmony and output.

Conflicts, while often seen as inhibitors, can be catalysts for collaboration if approached correctly. Emphasize the pursuit of mutual gains over individual victory. Equip your team with conflict resolution skills that galvanize relationships rather than fracturing them, turning potential setbacks into steps forward.

Invest in team building activities that go beyond the superficial. Delve into exercises that challenge your team to solve complex problems together, fortifying their collaborative muscles. These experiences are not only bonding but also serve as simulations for real-world scenarios, preparing your team to work seamlessly.

Technology has provided a plethora of tools designed to support collaboration. From project management platforms to communication applications, leverage these tools to keep your team connected and informed. However, remember that technology should enhance, not replace, the human element of teamwork.

In the orchestration of tasks, remember that autonomy is a powerful motivator. Allow team members to take ownership of their contributions within the collaborative process. When people feel a sense of individual responsibility coupled with collective accountability, engagement and productivity soar.

Keep in mind that fostering an inclusive environment is crucial to collaboration. Inclusivity means all voices are not only allowed but encouraged. When inclusivity is woven into the fabric of team operations, the result is a richer tapestry of ideas and solutions, exemplifying true synergy.

As a leader, being an exemplar of collaboration is non-negotiable. Serve as a mirror reflecting the behavior you want to see in your team. Your consistent demonstration of collaborative spirit shapes the norm, creating a ripple effect throughout the group.

Don't overlook the importance of celebrating collaborative wins, no matter the scale. Acknowledging and highlighting team achievements fuels motivation and reinforces the value of working in unison. Celebrations act as embers, keeping the team's spirit ignited and eager for future collaborations.

Finally, continuously assess and fine-tune the collaborative process within your team. Like a garden, the conditions that foster growth need regular nurturing and sometimes, a change in strategy. Collect feedback, observe interactions, and be prepared to evolve your approach to meet the dynamic needs of team synergy.

Embarking on the path of facilitating collaboration and team synergy isn't just about achieving outcomes; it's about crafting a journey that empowers individuals and solidifies the collective. When the synergy within your team resonates, it not only elevates projects to unprecedented heights but also leaves an indelible mark on each member, your leadership, and the organization at large.

Chapter 10:
Leveraging Diversity for Innovative Leadership

In today's increasingly interconnected world, the tapestry of the workforce is more diverse than ever before. As we transition from fostering collaboration and team synergy, it's imperative to recognize that innovation thrives at the intersection of varied experiences, perspectives, and life stories. Embracing such diversity isn't just the right thing to do; it becomes a strategic differentiator for the astute leader. When diverse voices contribute to a shared goal, the results are astounding—solutions are more robust, creativity is amplified, and organizational agility soars. Clever leaders understand that to harness the full potential of their teams, they must create an environment where every individual's unique strengths are recognized and leveraged. This isn't just about meeting a checklist of inclusivity benchmarks; it's about weaving a rich tapestry where each thread plays a pivotal role in the strength and beauty of the final product. By implementing inclusive leadership strategies, we can cultivate a culture that not only accepts diversity but thrives on it, unlocking unprecedented levels of innovation and leadership excellence.

Understanding the Value of Diversity

In the vibrant tapestry of modern leadership, the value of diversity emerges as a central thread that, when woven into the organizational fabric, enhances its strength, versatility, and beauty. Diversity in this context expands well beyond the traditional boundaries of race and

72

gender—it encompasses a broad spectrum of thought, experience, cultural background, age, personality, and much more.

Diverse teams are often hallmarked by a richness of perspectives that cultivate innovative problem-solving and creative thinking. The different life stories each member brings to the table serve as a wellspring for out-of-the-box ideas and unique approaches. Imagine a think tank, where every suggestion is uniquely shaped by varied experiences and knowledge, converging to form a collective intelligence that is far superior to uniform thought.

Leaders who grasp the intrinsic value of this diversity set the stage for an environment where these differences are not just present but are genuinely celebrated. This celebration fosters a sense of belonging and value among team members, fueling their motivation and propulsion towards achieving common goals. When people feel that their unique perspectives are acknowledged and appreciated, they're far more likely to bring their whole selves to the task at hand, unlocking the doors to passion and engagement.

Leveraging diversity is akin to conducting an orchestra, where every instrument plays a distinct sound. It is the role of the leader, much like the conductor, to blend these different notes harmoniously, creating a symphony that could never be realized through homogeneity. In doing so, it's important to appreciate not only the music from each instrument but also the potential for harmony between them.

Communication in diverse teams can be more challenging yet markedly rewarding. Differences in communication style can lead to misunderstandings or conflicts, but also to richer, multi-layered dialogues. Nurturing an environment where open, respectful communication is the norm is key. Here, each person is encouraged to share their viewpoint, voice their concerns, and know they will be heard.

It's important to recognize that our inherent biases can cloud our ability to value diversity. Leaders need to cultivate self-awareness to recognize these biases and actively work against them. By setting personal examples and encouraging others to do the same, a leader can gradually shift perceptions within the team, making it more inclusive and open-minded.

The allure of diversity extends to the market as well. A diverse team is better equipped to understand and respond to the needs of a global marketplace. Employees from different backgrounds bring insights into cultural norms and consumer behavior that can guide a company to navigate international waters with finesse and resonates more genuinely with a diverse client base.

Moreover, diversity can be the bedrock of innovation. When team members with various backgrounds and experiences collaborate, the fusion of their distinct thought processes can lead to the kind of innovative solutions that propel companies forward. Such innovation is the lifeblood of competitive advantage in today's fast-paced economy.

But diversity must be more than just a buzzword; it requires commitment from leadership to embed these values into the organization's DNA. Leaders must not only recruit for diversity but must also nurture an inclusive environment that empowers all voices. It is the proactive steps to ensure all employees have equal opportunities for development and growth that truly unleashes the potential of a diverse workforce.

It is also about resilience. Diversity within teams brings multiple coping strategies and varied approaches to problem-solving. Thus, when faced with setbacks or challenges, these teams are better equipped to pivot and adapt. They draw strength from their multitude of experiences to find pathways through the most daunting of obstacles.

Building a culture that values diversity also means acknowledging and mitigating the systemic barriers that have historically marginalized certain groups. This level of authentic commitment can resonate across the team, inspiring trust and loyalty, which are indispensable for long-term sustainability and success.

Leaders must also understand the intricacies of equity—the fair treatment, access, and advancement for all individuals. While equality means giving everyone the same resources, equity involves distributing resources based on the needs of the individuals. By embracing equity, leaders ensure that every team member can contribute to their full potential.

To foster such an environment, leaders must be intentional about team dynamics. It's not enough to bring diverse individuals together; leaders must encourage interaction, collaboration, and mutual learning. Structured team-building activities and regular check-ins can help bridge gaps between team members and promote a more cohesive unit.

Finally, recognizing and celebrating the achievements of a diverse team can serve as a powerful motivator. It reaffirms the organization's commitment to an inclusive culture and highlights the tangible benefits of diverse collaboration. Through recognition, leaders reinforce the message that each person's contribution is vital to the team's success, thereby promoting an atmosphere where diversity continues to thrive.

In summation, understanding the value of diversity is to acknowledge its foundational role in shaping teams that are robust, adaptable, and innovative. It's about creating spaces where differences illuminate new paths and where diverse voices collectively chart the course to success. For leaders aspiring to inspire, motivate, and guide their teams toward unparalleled achievements, embracing diversity is not merely an ethical imperative but a strategic mastery that can steer their ship through the often tumultuous waters of the competitive business world.

Strategies for Inclusive Leadership

In the realm of innovative leadership, diversity isn't just a buzzword; it's a catalyst for breakthroughs and unrivaled creativity. As leaders, fostering an environment where every voice is heard and valued is not just about fairness; it's a strategic imperative. Inclusive leadership is the beacon that draws out the full spectrum of talent and perspectives within your team.

At the heart of inclusive leadership is respect and openness. Begin by taking deliberate steps to understand cultural differences and how they shape interactions and expectations. Knowledge is foundational, but it's the application that builds bridges. Engage in conversations with your team members to learn about their unique experiences and viewpoints. This isn't merely an exercise in socialization; it's an investment in trust and understanding.

A truly inclusive leader takes the time to reflect critically on their own biases and preconceptions. We all have them, but what separates leaders is the courage to confront and overcome these barriers. By doing so, you'll not only inspire but also empower your team to bring their authentic selves to work. The ripple effect of authenticity can energize an entire organization.

But understanding isn't enough if it doesn't translate into practice. Make inclusivity tangible in your decision-making processes. Diverse teams might find consensus a challenge, but the solutions born from their deliberation tend to be more robust and innovative. Welcome different standpoints and use these as a launchpad for exploring new ideas and approaches.

Effective communication is another cornerstone of inclusive leadership. Tailor your communication style to ensure clarity and understanding across a diverse team. This might involve simplifying language, removing jargon, or providing context. Remember, the intent is not to dilute messages but to ensure they resonate with everyone, regardless of background.

Visibility and representation matter. As an inclusive leader, work toward ensuring every layer of the organization reflects the diversity of the teams they oversee. Representation can't stop at entry-level positions. It needs to echo up through the ranks, ensuring that diversity is not only present but thriving at all organizational levels.

Developing cultural intelligence within your team is an endeavor that pays dividends. Encourage your team to familiarize themselves with each other's backgrounds and cultures. Cultivate an environment where cultural exchange is as routine as morning meetings. The empathy and insight gained from this practice contribute to a richer, more inclusive team dynamic.

Inclusion is also about accessibility. Is everyone in your team equipped with the tools and opportunities to succeed? Consider practices and technologies that accommodate different abilities and working styles. From offering flexible work arrangements to ensuring physical spaces are accessible to all, inclusivity in practice is about removing barriers to participation and success.

Rethink how you recognize and reward success within your team. Celebrating achievements is crucial, but an inclusive leader knows to value the diverse ways in which success can manifest. Some may achieve through outspoken leadership, others through quiet support and diligence. Recognize the spectrum of excellence and shine a light on varied contributions.

Mentorship and sponsorship are two powerful tools in the inclusive leader's arsenal. Identify potential in individuals who may not fit the traditional mold of leadership and offer them opportunities for growth. Pairing emerging leaders with experienced mentors can help bridge gaps in experience while sponsorship can thrust them into new opportunities they might not have otherwise had access to.

Embracing alternative perspectives in problem-solving fosters a culture where challenges are welcomed as opportunities to innovate. Encourage teams to deconstruct problems and reconstruct solutions that benefit from the best that diverse thinking offers. When a team knows that their unique perspective is valued, they'll be more willing to contribute their ideas freely and passionately.

Feedback is a two-way street in an inclusive leadership model. It's not enough to provide guidance; you must be open to receiving it from all levels of your organization. Create channels for feedback that allow your team to express their thoughts on leadership and operational practices without fear of repercussions. This transparency can lead to critical improvements and increased trust.

Avoiding exclusionary practices requires vigilance and action. Regularly assess your team's dynamics, processes, and outcomes for signs of exclusion or marginalization. This is not a once-and-done check; it's a continuous commitment to ensuring your leadership adapts and aligns with the values of inclusivity and respect.

Finally, celebrate the varied tapestry of your team's composition. Make it known that diversity isn't just tolerated; it's desired. Highlight stories of collaborative success stemming from diverse partnerships within your organization. Let these stories become part of your team's identity, something they can all take pride in and strive to contribute to.

In the journey towards inclusive leadership, the path is not always linear, and challenges are inevitable. However, every step taken to promote diversity and inclusion elevates not only your leadership but the entire organization. Inclusivity is more than just a strategic advantage; it's a commitment to excellence, a bridge to innovation, and a declaration that every person holds intrinsic value within your team.

Chapter 11:
Continuous Improvement and Lifelong Learning

As we turn the page from understanding the dynamics of diverse, innovative teams, let's pivot to an essential cornerstone of effective leadership: the commitment to continuous improvement and lifelong learning. Embarking on this journey requires an unshakable belief in the potential for growth—both in ourselves and in those we lead. Imagine a work culture where every challenge is seen not as an obstacle but as a stepping stone to greater knowledge and capability. Envision the ripple effect as each individual's personal development fuels the team's evolution, crafting an environment where progress is the norm, not the exception. With every insight gained and skill honed, leaders must reinforce the cycle, celebrating milestones while encouraging the pursuit of mastery that extends beyond the office walls. This virtuous circle of learning resoundingly echoes in the quality of work, the vibrancy of collaborations, and the innovation that springs from a team confident in its ability to adapt and flourish. So, as we delve into the fibers of continuous improvement and lifelong learning, let's commit to igniting a passion for perpetual growth that illuminates the path to exceptional leadership.

Fostering a Growth Mindset

Within the kaleidoscope of leadership and motivation, nurturing a growth mindset stands out as a transformative ethos. It shifts leaders and their teams from the rigidity of a 'fixed' mindset to the dynamism and potential of continual evolution. A growth mindset opens up a universe of possibilities where challenges become opportunities for personal and professional development rather than insurmountable obstacles.

To embrace a growth mindset, leaders need to first internalize the concept that abilities and intelligence can be developed. This simple yet profound belief has the power to ignite an unwavering commitment to learning and improvement—not just within oneself but also within the teams they lead. As a leader, celebrating efforts, strategizing around mistakes, and valuing potential will all echo loudly in the halls of your organization.

Lest we forget, fostering a growth mindset isn't just about praising hard work. It encompasses an ability to recognize and reinforce effort, strategy, and progress. Encourage your team to take intellectual risks by stepping outside of their comfort zones. It's within this space that real growth germinates, as people challenge their own limits and learn from outcomes, regardless of success or failure.

Embodying a growth mindset also means steering through the landscape of constructive criticism effectively. By delivering feedback that focuses on processes and strategies, rather than personal traits, you'll foster resilience and a passion for learning in your team. This method supports individuals in understanding that their performance can and will improve with effort and time.

Remember, setting the benchmark for a growth mindset starts with you, the leader. Your credibility hinges on how well you demonstrate an openness to learning and an appetite for feedback. Be transparent about your own learning journey. Share your reflections on failures and how they've been integral to your development. Your vulnerability can be a powerful catalyst for trust and inspiration.

Astutely, the growth mindset isn't just a mental exercise but an actionable practice. Integrate new challenges into the routine, encourage creative problem-solving, and recognize innovative solutions. By doing so, you create an environment where continuous improvement is not only encouraged but expected.

Moving forward, set the stage for open communication. Foster an atmosphere where team members feel comfortable voicing their thoughts, questions, and ideas. It's through this dialogue that a collective intelligence emerges, one that dissipates the fear of failure and celebrates the process of learning.

Moreover, instigate a reflection culture within your team. Prompt them to consistently reflect on their experiences, distilling lessons and insights from every project or task. These retrospectives aren't just for appraising success but, importantly, for unearthing the wisdom in hiccups and missteps.

Also, take a proactive role in your team's development by providing resources for learning. Whether it's access to online courses, workshops, or time set aside for innovation, these tools are the building blocks of a knowledge-rich atmosphere where a growth mindset can thrive.

Let's not underestimate the role of recognition in reinforcing a growth mindset. Genuine acknowledgment of growth-oriented behaviors alleviates the fear of inadequacy and reinforces the fact that the path of improvement is valued as highly as the result itself.

Aligning individual objectives with organizational goals is another key strategy. Help your team members understand how their personal development furthers the collective mission. Seeing one's role in the larger tapestry of the organization can be a potent motivator for continual growth and contribution.

As new tasks and projects are undertaken, remember to iterate on strategies and processes with your team. Involve them in the conversation about what can be done better next time. This iterative approach exemplifies the very essence of a growth mindset—acknowledging that there is always room for improvement.

In the end, fostering a growth mindset is a conscious choice and an ongoing endeavor. It's a commitment to seeing potential, nurturing curiosity, and understanding that mastery is a perpetually evolving journey. Acknowledge that growth is a route marked by persistence and learning from every step, not merely reaching a destination.

To encapsulate, cultivating a growth mindset within your team is pivotal for fostering an environment of continuous improvement and lifelong learning. It is the invisible thread that weaves through every aspect of leadership and motivation, strengthening the resolve to flourish amidst the certainty of change.

And so, as you write the narrative of your leadership story, let the ink be infused with the values of a growth mindset. Let each page reflect an unyielding belief in the boundless potential of yourself and those you lead, for it is within this mindset that the most compelling chapters of success are composed.

Implementing Continuous Feedback Mechanisms

In our pursuit of excellence and growth, it's critical to recognize that feedback is not just a tool, it is the cornerstone of continuous improvement. Implementing continuous feedback mechanisms within your team or organization is a transformative strategy that empowers individuals, encourages learning, and fosters a culture of open communication and perpetual progress.

To start, we must recognize that feedback loops are vital for correcting course and celebrating achievements. Imagine a rudderless ship; without feedback, direction is lost. As a leader, it is essential that you establish robust channels of communication where feedback flows freely and constructively.

One of the first steps in crafting these feedback mechanisms is to define what success looks like. This provides a clear benchmark against which feedback can be measured. Clarity in goals and expectations aligns team efforts and makes feedback more relevant and actionable.

It's also about creating an environment where feedback is normalized. This means cultivating a space where team members feel comfortable sharing their insights without fear of repercussion. Make it known that each voice is valued and that feedback is a means to drive collective success, not a punitive measure.

The frequency of feedback is as critical as its quality. Regular check-ins keep the team engaged and on track. Consider implementing weekly or bi-weekly one-on-one meetings where you can provide real-time, specific feedback that recognizes accomplishments and addresses challenges promptly.

Technology offers a powerful platform for continuous feedback. Utilize digital tools that allow for anonymous surveys, real-time reactions, and platforms where praise can be shared and achievements recognized. These tools break down the barriers of time and location, ensuring feedback is an ongoing process rather than an annual event.

To amplify the power of feedback, make it a two-way street. Invite team members to give feedback about leadership and organizational practices. This not only enhances trust but also provides valuable insights that can propel leadership effectiveness and organizational growth.

Feedback should also be concrete and behavior-based. Instead of vague comments like 'Good job,' detail what exactly was done well, such as 'Your detailed report provided valuable insights that helped us make an informed decision.' This specificity makes feedback more meaningful and provides a clear path for replication and improvement.

Training on giving and receiving feedback is also pivotal. Equip your team with the skills to communicate their thoughts effectively and to receive feedback with an open mind. When individuals view feedback as an opportunity for growth rather than criticism, the entire organization benefits.

Actionability is a key element of effective feedback. Each piece of feedback should be accompanied by suggestions for improvement or plans for reinforcement of positive behaviors. Without a path forward, feedback can feel aimless and demotivating.

It's paramount to close the feedback loop. Acknowledge when changes have been made in response to feedback and make sure the outcomes of those changes are shared with the team. This reassures everyone that their contributions have weight and that their efforts to evolve are recognized.

Including peer feedback can also be a valuable component, promoting accountability and camaraderie among team members. This peer-to-peer feedback nurtures a supportive environment where individuals learn from each other and grow together.

Tracking progress over time through consistent feedback allows team members to see their evolution and instills a sense of accomplishment. When people can map their growth, it energizes them to continue pushing their boundaries and elevates their motivation to learn.

Lastly, remember that feedback should be a celebration of the journey as much as it is a tool for improvement. Recognizing the steps forward, no matter how small, invigorates the team and emboldens them to reach for ever-greater heights. After all, the pillars of motivation are built upon the recognition of progress and success.

Continuous feedback mechanisms are the heartbeat of an organization striving for excellence. By implementing these strategies in your leadership practice, you're not just driving performance; you're nurturing an environment where continuous improvement and lifelong learning are ingrained in the very fabric of your team's culture. In doing so, you create a legacy—a team that is resilient, adaptable, and unwavering in its pursuit of growth and excellence.

Chapter 12:
Navigating Change and Uncertainty

In the flux of the modern world, a leader's ability to navigate change and uncertainty isn't just ideal – it's imperative. As we turn the page from the rudiments of continuous growth and learning, we encounter the unpredictable waves that leadership must surf with grace. In this chapter, we delve into harnessing the inevitable force of change and using it to fuel our leadership journey. We look at strategies to lead teams through the vortex of transformation with a steady hand, all while fostering an environment that's not just robust but thrives on the inevitable shifts that life throws our way. Change should be worn as armor, not avoided. By cultivating an adaptive team culture and equipping our teams with tools to pivot with agility, we build fortresses capable of withstanding any storm. The expertise laid out in this chapter is a map through the fog, a beacon to transforming uncertainty into a compass, guiding us towards new horizons in our leadership odyssey.

Leading Through Change

The winds of change are relentless, and as a leader, sailing these tempestuous seas requires a steadfast hand and an unwavering vision. Change can come from technology, market shifts, or within the organization itself. To navigate these uncertain waters, leaders must foster resilience and adaptability, while also maintaining a focus on the human side of transformation.

Leadership, in the face of change, is about more than steering the organization through new strategies and processes. It's about understanding the emotional journey your team embarks upon. Every change brings with it a spectrum of reactions; from excitement and opportunity to fear and resistance. You, as a leader, must be the compass that guides your team through their individual responses, maintaining an environment where motivation thrives amidst the unknown.

Communication is the linchpin during periods of change. It can't be overstated how essential clear, consistent, and transparent dialogue is. Your team looks to you to demystify the future, to make sense of the shifting landscape. It's important to share information openly and create forums where questions are encouraged, ideas are aired, and concerns are addressed.Remember, silence breeds skepticism—it's in the narrative void that rumors and fear can take root.

When leading through change, your personal vision can be a beacon, but so too can the collective vision of your team. Engaging your team in shaping the vision not only empowers them but also imparts a sense of ownership over the change process. This shared vision functions as a driving force that aligns the team's actions and maintains a high level of motivation and commitment to the objective ahead.

Expect and plan for resistance to change. It's a natural human reaction to the unfamiliar and uncertain. Acknowledging this resistance is the first step in addressing it. Understanding the underlying concerns allows you to provide the necessary support and training to ease the transition. Transform resistance into readiness by highlighting the benefits and facilitating a smooth journey from the old to the new.

Change often requires learning new skills or adjusting existing ones. Investing in your team's development during times of change is critical. Training and development are not just about capability but are powerful motivational tools. They demonstrate your commitment to your team's growth, which in turn, enhances their dedication to the change initiative.

As a change leader, your adaptability sets the tone for your team. Demonstrate flexibility in your approaches and be open to feedback. Change isn't always linear; it requires the ability to pivot when necessary. When you model adaptability, you give permission for your team to do the same, creating a dynamic and responsive environment. This showcases leadership that is not just authoritative but also collaborative and responsive to the needs of the moment.

In the midst of change, it's crucial to acknowledge achievements along the way. Recognize both small wins and major milestones as part of the journey. This practice of recognition nurtures a positive atmosphere and keeps the team's spirits high. It is these moments of acknowledgement that can recharge motivation, reminding everyone involved that progress is being made, and their efforts are valued.

Promoting a sense of resilience within your team is just as fundamental as any strategy you deploy. Resilience enables individuals and teams to rebound from setbacks and persist in the face of challenges. You can cultivate this by sharing stories of past successes, providing resources to bolster coping skills, and encouraging a mindset that sees obstacles as opportunities for growth and learning.

The ultimate test of leadership during change is how you handle failure. Not every initiative will go as planned, and mistakes are inevitable. Your reaction to these setbacks will either fuel fear or inspire persistence. Embrace failure as a learning opportunity. When you do so, you send a powerful message that it's okay to take risks and that growth often occurs at the edge of our comfort zones.

Empathy during times of change is what differentiates a leader from a manager. Understand that change can be disorienting and stressful for your team. Be present, be human, and connect with them on an emotional level. It's this empathy that will build trust and loyalty, making your team willing to follow you, even when the path is uncertain.

To lead effectively through change, self-care is not a luxury—it's a necessity. Change can be as draining for the leader as it is for the team. Be mindful of your own well-being, as it impacts your ability to be present and positive for those you guide. Taking care of yourself ensures you have the energy and clarity to support others.

Finally, practice patience. Change is a process, not an event. It takes time for individuals and organizations to internalize new ways of working. Patience allows you to recognize that each person's journey through change will be unique and to provide the tailored support they need. Your steady presence throughout the process is a testament to leadership that not only directs but also cares and connects.

As you lead your team through the ebbs and flows of change, remember that what you are ultimately doing is setting the precedent for how change is embraced within the culture of your organization. Your actions, your demeanor, and your guidance are crafting a narrative of change that will be referred to long after the current transition is a distant memory. This is your legacy as a leader: not merely where you steer the ship, but how you inspire your crew during the voyage.

Embrace this journey with confidence, knowing that the tools you've honed and the strategies you implement are the catalysts for transformation. Leadership through change is one of the most profound opportunities to shape the future—not just of your organization, but of the people who make it what it is. Stand firm in your conviction, agile in your approach, and compassionate in your leadership, and you'll not only navigate change, you'll catalyze it.

Building Adaptive and Agile Teams

Change is the only constant in our hyper-connected world, and the ability to navigate this evolving landscape defines a leader's calibre. As stewards of growth and innovation, your role is to construct teams not just capable of adapting to change, but thriving within it. This means fostering agility—a blend of flexibility, balance, and coordination that is reflected in decision-making and execution.

To build an adaptive and agile team, you start by selecting individuals with diverse skill sets and cognitive approaches. A team varied in expertise and perspective is better equipped to handle a breadth of challenges. Then, invest in these individuals, cross-training them to develop their skills beyond their core competencies. This creates a dynamic workforce that can pivot as circumstances demand.

Agility thrives on open communication. Foster an environment where ideas are freely exchanged and where team members feel comfortable voicing concerns and suggesting improvements. Such transparency sows the seeds of trust and is a critical element in responsive decision-making.

Leaders must also demonstrate adaptability. Show your team that you can advocate for new strategies when old ones falter. Be a model of resilience; when a leader recovers gracefully and learns from failure, it encourages the team to adopt a similar resilient ethic.

Empowering teams also means decentralizing command. Give team members autonomy over their tasks and decision-making authority appropriate to their roles. This not only builds confidence but also allows for quicker responses to change since decisions do not have to pass through a bottleneck at the leadership level.

Understanding the strengths of each team member enables you to delegate effectively. Assign roles that play to those strengths, and challenge each member to take on stretch tasks that push them to innovate and grow. This approach leverages intrinsic motivation, which fosters a more engaged and productive team.

Encourage a mindset that views challenges as opportunities for growth. When teams adopt a positive perception of change, they're more likely to approach it with creativity and enthusiasm. Drive this mindset by celebrating both the big victories and small wins, showing that progress in any measure is valuable.

Learning from failure is invaluable for an agile team. Encourage a culture where mishaps are dissected for learning, not punished. This not only refines processes but also reinforces psychological safety, ensuring team members aren't paralyzed by the fear of failure.

Rapid prototyping and feedback loops are indispensable in an agile environment. Implement systems that allow for quick development cycles and iterative testing. This enables your team to refine solutions in real time, adapt to feedback and evolve continually towards the most effective outcome.

When it comes to planning, emphasize flexibility over rigid adherence to plans that may become obsolete. Train teams to identify key decision points and to pivot as needed, rather than following a predetermined path that may lead to obsolescence.

Agility is complemented by a penchant for proactive learning. Cultivate an atmosphere of continuous skill development, encouraging your team to stay ahead of industry trends and technological advancements. This ensures your team will not just respond to the next challenge but anticipate it.

Metrics and benchmarks are crucial, but in the agile framework, they should not be fixed. Set adaptable performance indicators that evolve with the project and progress. This allows teams to measure success in a way that acknowledges their learning and growth over time.

Remember, the core of team agility is not merely surviving change, but using it as a springboard for innovation and improvement. This means sometimes foregoing the safe route for the one that offers growth, even if it poses more substantial challenges.

Lastly, provide your team with the tools and technologies that support agile practices. Up-to-date resources can streamline processes, facilitate collaboration, and enable better management of complex projects in a fast-paced environment.

Building adaptive and agile teams requires vision, intentionality, and a consistent commitment to growth and flexibility. As a leader, nurture these qualities within your team, and watch as they transform challenges into opportunities, driving success even amidst uncertainty. With an adaptive and agile team, you're poised not just to react to the future, but to shape it.

Chapter 13:
Leadership as a Lifelong Journey

The leadership landscape, with its peaks and valleys, offers an endless path of discovery and growth. As we conclude this exploration of leadership and motivation, it's crucial to acknowledge an essential truth: the journey of leadership doesn't have a final destination. It is a continuous trek—an evolution that challenges you to climb higher, delve deeper, and push beyond the familiar boundaries of comfort and certainty.

Throughout this book, we've navigated the intricate dance of leading and motivating, unfurling the layers that constitute effective, dynamic leadership. The characteristics of leadership we've dissected—emotional intelligence, communication, goal-setting, positive reinforcement, and more—are not items on a checklist to be marked off and forgotten. Instead, they are the interwoven threads of a tapestry that is never fully complete.

As you stand on the threshold of tomorrow, armed with the insights and strategies from these chapters, it's important to recognize the fluidity of leading. Every encounter, every challenge, every triumph is an opportunity to refine your skills and adapt your approach. The most successful leaders are those who embrace growth as a staple of their existence, not just an occasional adjustment when problems arise.

This path you are walking is one of perpetual learning. As each day unfolds, you will discover new facets of your leadership style and new dimensions of your team's capabilities. The goal setting and goal-getting you've mastered is not a linear loop but a spiral, expanding and evolving with each rotation. In your journey, there will be missteps; accept these as gifts—priceless lessons that enrich your wisdom and resilience.

Remember the importance of fostering a positive organizational culture—one where motivation thrives and every member feels valued. The work environment you shape today lays the groundwork for the leaders of tomorrow. By leading by example and modeling the behaviors you wish to see, you become a living blueprint for others to follow, inspiring new generations to elevate the standards of leadership.

Your vision and the purpose you communicate will be your North Star, guiding your actions and illuminating your path. Keep them close to your heart, relentless in your pursuit, but flexible in your execution. The role you play as a leader is not just about reaching the targets you've set; it's about the legacy of inspiration and encouragement you leave in your wake.

The teams you develop, the collaborations you foster, and the synergies you facilitate are all part of the continual process of becoming an impactful leader. Each person you lead—and every life you touch—adds a unique brushstroke to the canvas of your leadership journey, creating a masterpiece that is ever-expanding and eternally beautiful.

In the realm of diversity, let the myriad perspectives and ideas fuel your innovative spirit. Inclusivity isn't merely a box to tick; it's a lens through which to see the world, a strategy for uncovering hidden opportunities, and a method to harness the full potential of the collective genius that diversity offers.

Champion the growth mindset in yourself and in your team. See each challenge not as a setback but as a setup for a breakthrough. Cultivate a love of learning, for the leaders who thrive are those who never stop querying, questioning, and questing for knowledge. The implementation of continuous feedback loops ensures that this mindset becomes part of your team's DNA, propelling you all toward excellence.

In the face of change and uncertainty, stand unwavering in your commitment to guide your team with courage and clarity. Develop agility not just in thought, but in action. Build a team that adapts with grace, that views the unexpected not with trepidation but with a thrill of opportunity. The unknown is not a specter to fear, but a horizon to meet.

As your leadership journey unfolds, commit to revisiting the tools and strategies provided in these pages often. The appendices at the end of this book are there to support your development, providing resources, self-assessment tools, and motivation techniques to revisit and adapt as you grow.

Perhaps the most profound realization you will come to on this journey is that leadership is not a role to be played but a life to be lived. It is not about the title before your name or the accolades that follow it; it is about the difference you make, the lives you enhance, and the vision you bring to life. Look within and around you, draw on your strengths, learn from the world, and lead with heart.

And so, with a sense of humble anticipation, let us part at this juncture—knowing that, although this book may close, your voyage as a leader burgeons anew each day. Continue to walk this road with purpose, passion, and perseverance. Embrace the complexities, celebrate the triumphs, learn from the lessons, and always move forward. Leadership, after all, is a lifelong journey—one that reveals its treasures to those who dare to travel its path with an open heart and an eager spirit.

Appendix A:
Resources for Further Learning

Embarking on your journey as a transformational leader is a commitment to perpetual growth and learning. As you continue to explore and refine your leadership capabilities, an array of resources stands ready to serve as companions in your quest for excellence. This appendix is hand-crafted to provide you with a wellspring of knowledge and inspiration that supplements your leadership journey and your quest in mastering the art of motivation.

Books and Publications

The vast world of literature offers countless insights into the human psyche, motivation, and effective leadership. Seek out books that not only provide theoretical frameworks but also share practical applications and real-life case studies. From timeless classics to contemporary works, a diverse reading list can broaden your perspective and deepen your understanding of what it means to lead and inspire.

- **Inspirational Biographies:** Through the lives of great leaders, learn the essence of resilience, vision, and influence.

- **Leadership and Management Theories:** Delve into books that break down the mechanics of leadership and the science of motivation.

- **Cultural and Emotional Intelligence:** Equip yourself with the tools to navigate the complex human elements at the core of leading diverse teams.

Online Courses and Workshops

Interactive learning experiences allow you to put theory into practice. Online platforms offer a plethora of courses that cater to different aspects of leadership, communication, and team motivation. Look for workshops that include practical exercises, opportunities for reflective practice, and even peer collaboration that can mimic real-world leadership scenarios.

- **Leadership Development Programs:** Structured courses often offer a comprehensive curriculum to enhance specific leadership skills.

- **Communication Mastery Classes:** Focus on courses that hone your ability to listen, empathize, and communicate with impact.

- **Team Building Seminars:** Learn the dynamics of successful team development and strategies to foster collaboration.

Podcasts and Webinars

In a fast-paced world, podcasts and webinars offer the luxury of learning on-the-go. These platforms provide access to thought leaders and innovators' insights without the confines of structured classes. Subscribe to channels that focus on leadership trends, motivational strategies, and workplace culture to stay updated and inspired.

- **Leadership Thought Leader Series:** Get into the minds of successful leaders through interviews and discussions.

- **Team Motivation Podcasts:** Discover various motivational techniques and success stories to implement in your team.

- **Culture Building Webinars:** Learn from experts about creating an organizational culture that breathes motivation.

Networking and Professional Groups

Building a network of peers and mentors is crucial in leadership development. Join relevant professional groups, forums, or associations that allow you to connect, share experiences, and learn from others' journeys. Often, the collective wisdom of a group can illuminate solutions to complex challenges and inspire new ideas.

- **Leadership Forums:** Engage in discussions and build connections with fellow leaders across industries.

- **Mastermind Groups:** Partner with a group dedicated to mutual growth, accountability, and support.

- **Professional Associations:** Participate in organizations specific to your industry to gain tailored insights and practices.

- Remember, the craft of leadership is never static; it flourishes with every interaction, every decision, and every challenge you embrace. The resources outlined here serve as a lighthouse, guiding you through the uncharted waters of leadership and motivation. Keep the flame of curiosity kindled, and let it be the beacon that propels you to new horizons in your leadership journey.

Appendix B:
Self-Assessment Tools for Leaders

Embarking on the leadership journey calls for a deep understanding of oneself. As a leader, your growth and development are predicated on self-awareness and a willingness to adapt and evolve. Self-assessment tools are invaluable resources that provide insights into your leadership style, strengths, and areas for improvement.

Finding Your Leadership Style

One of the first steps in utilizing self-assessment tools is to decipher your leadership style. This understanding will enable you to align your approach with the needs of your team and the objectives of your organization. To determine your style, consider reflecting on how you handle decisions, conflict, and communication. Are you more of a democratic leader who values the team's input, or do you lean towards an autocratic style, preferring to make decisions unilaterally? Perhaps you find yourself exhibiting transformational qualities, inspiring others with a compelling vision for the future.

Emotional Intelligence (EI) Assessment

Emotional intelligence is the cornerstone of effective leadership. It's about understanding your emotions and those of others to foster strong relationships and make informed decisions. To assess your EI, look for tools that measure key components such as self-awareness, self-regulation, motivation, empathy, and social skills. These components are essential for leaders who aim not just to manage, but to motivate and elevate their team members.

Strengths and Weaknesses Analysis

Understanding your strengths and weaknesses is vital in honing your leadership capabilities. Conduct an honest evaluation of where you excel and where there's room for growth. This can take the form of self-reflection, peer feedback, or more structured tools like SWOT analysis, which can be personalized for individual development.

Motivation Potential Assessment

As a leader, your role is to motivate others, but what motivates you? Assessing your own drivers through tools that explore intrinsic and extrinsic motivation can shed light on how you can inspire yourself and, in turn, inspire others. Knowing what fuels your passion for leadership will keep you engaged and committed to your role.

Communication Skills Inventory

Effective leaders are also effective communicators. Use self-assessment tools that evaluate your listening, verbal, and non-verbal communication skills. These tools can pinpoint areas where you can improve your clarity, empathy, and ability to connect with others, all of which are crucial in leading successfully.

Conflict Resolution Quotient

Leaders must be adept at dealing with conflicts. Explore assessments that help you understand your conflict resolution style. Are you an avoider, collaborator, competitor, accommodator, or compromiser?

Knowing your natural inclinations in conflict situations can help you to develop more balanced approaches.

Goal-Setting and Achievement Gauge

The way you set and achieve goals can significantly impact your effectiveness. Use tools that help you analyze your goal-setting strategies, such as whether you gravitate toward SMART goals or if you might benefit from alternative frameworks. This self-assessment can guide you toward refining your ability to set, pursue, and reach impactful goals for you and your team.

In your hands, these tools are more than just assessments; they are a compass that guides your continual growth as a leader. They invite introspection and incite a transformation that resonates through the entirety of your team, sparking motivation, fostering resilience, and cultivating a thriving organizational culture. Embrace these tools with an open heart and a growth mindset, and watch as the seeds of effective leadership take root and flourish within you.

Appendix C:
Motivation Techniques Repository

Enlightening leadership isn't simply a matter of intention; it's an art form anchored in the subtleties of human motivation. This chapter, like a well-organized palette, serves as a repository of motivation techniques, offering new leaders a spectrum of strategies to inspire their teams and foster an environment where motivation can flourish organically.

Arsenal of Inspiration

Leadership demands versatility in our approach to motivation, recognizing that no single strategy fits all scenarios. Herein lies a categorized tapestry of motivation techniques, ready to be woven into the fabric of daily leadership.

- **Empowerment through Autonomy** - Provide team members the freedom to choose "how" to accomplish their tasks, igniting a sense of ownership and responsibility.

- **Goals That Galvanize** - Collaboratively set vivid, challenging yet attainable goals that urge your team to stretch their capabilities and imagine new possibilities.

- **Recognition and Praise** - A timely Word of affirmation can act as a catalyst for continued excellence and commitment.

- **Personalized Encouragement** - Tailor your support to the individual's needs, acknowledging their unique contributions and professional aspirations.

- **Constructive Feedback** - Offer feedback that shapes growth, subtly guiding your team towards greater achievements and personal development.

Stoking the Fire Within

The cornerstone of enduring motivation is the spark that burns from within each team member. To stoke these inner fires, consider these internal motivators:

- **Shared Purpose** - Cultivate a shared vision that aligns personal ambitions with the organization's purpose, creating a harmonious pursuit of objectives.

- **Masterful Skill Development** - Champion continuous learning, encouraging your team to master new skills that resonate with their career trajectory.

- **Challenge and Competence** - Design tasks that provide a balance between challenge and skill level, fostering a state of 'flow' where team members lose themselves in their work.

Creating a Culture of Motivation

As leaders, it's our prerogative to mold an atmosphere that breathes motivation:

- **Elevating Environments** - Establish an environment that supports and celebrates creativity, risk-taking, and the joy of shared success.

- **Progress Celebrations** - Recognize not only the destination but also the journey by commemorating milestones and incremental progress.

- **Transparency and Trust** - Build trust through transparency, demonstrating a commitment to honesty and open communication.

Motivation is the wind in the sails of our leadership. It propels our teams forward, coaxing out latent potential and driving collective achievement. The techniques outlined above are not exhaustive; they are starting points, seeds of inspiration from which your unique approach to leadership and motivation can grow. Wield these strategies with consideration, adaptability, and a keen awareness of your team's dynamics. It's through this personalized application that you will not just lead but truly elevate those around you, propelling your organization toward uncharted territories of success.

www.ingramcontent.com/pod-product-compliance
Lightning Source LLC
Chambersburg PA
CBHW022026170526
45157CB00003B/1366